77 Pasta Recipes for Home

By: Kelly Johnson

Table of Contents

Pastas:

- Spaghetti Bolognese
- Fettuccine Alfredo
- Penne alla Vodka
- Carbonara
- Pesto Pasta
- Shrimp Scampi Linguine
- Garlic Butter Pasta
- Chicken Parmesan Pasta
- Tomato Basil Pasta
- Aglio e Olio
- Cajun Chicken Pasta
- Primavera Pasta
- Lemon Garlic Shrimp Pasta
- Mushroom and Spinach Alfredo
- Baked Ziti
- Pasta Puttanesca
- Chicken Piccata Pasta
- Beef Stroganoff Pasta
- One-Pot Creamy Tuscan CHicken Pasta
- Broccoli Pesto Pasta
- Caprese Pasta Salad
- Goulash
- Mediterranean Pasta
- Shrimp and Broccoli Alfredo
- Chili Mac
- Creamy Sun-Dried Tomato Pasta
- Sausage and Peppers Pasta
- Lobster Ravioli
- Pasta e Fagioli
- Thai Peanut Noodles
- Spinach and Artichoke Pasta
- Chicken and Mushroom Fettuccine
- Butternut Squash Ravioli
- Lemon Ricotta Pasta
- Cacio e Pepe
- Taco Pasta
- Shrimp Fra Diavolo
- Avocado Pesto Pasta

- Chicken and Broccoli Alfredo
- Crab Linguine
- Spaghetti Aglio, Olio e Peperoncino
- Pumpkin Sage Pasta
- Mediterranean Orzo Salad
- Buffalo Chicken Mac and Cheese
- Chicken and Asparagus Lemon Pasta
- Rigatoni with Sausage and Kale
- Shrimp and Bacon Carbonara
- Lemon Butter Shrimp Pasta
- Mediterranean Vegetable Pasta
- Gnocchi with Brown Butter and Sage
- Chicken Marsala Pasta
- Shrimp and Avocado Pasta Salad
- Creamy Tomato and Basil Tortellini
- Baked Rigatoni with Meatballs
- Garlic Parmesan Pasta
- Sweet Potato Gnocchi
- Italian Sausage and Peppers Cavatappi
- Shrimp and Zucchini Noodles
- Roasted Red Pepper and Goat Cheese Pasta
- Chicken Alfredo Stuffed Shells
- Shrimp and Scallop Linguine
- Creamy Cajun Chicken and Sausage Pasta
- Pasta with Eggplant and Tomato Sauce
- Smoked Salmon and Dill Pasta
- Spaghetti with Clams
- Sun-Dried Tomato and Basil Pesto Pasta
- Beef and Mushroom Stuffed Shells
- Lemon Asparagus Orzo
- Pappardelle with Wild Mushroom Sauce
- Spaghetti Carbonara with Pancetta
- Creamy Tomato Basil Penne
- Chicken and Spinach Lasagna
- Broccoli and Cheddar Stuffed Shells
- Caramelized Onion and Goat Cheese Linguine
- Shrimp and Lobster Linguine
- Spicy Arrabbiata Pasta
- Creamy Pumpkin Alfredo

Spaghetti Bolognese

Ingredients:

- 1 pound (450g) ground beef
- 1 tablespoon olive oil
- 1 onion, finely chopped
- 2 carrots, finely chopped
- 2 celery stalks, finely chopped
- 3 cloves garlic, minced
- 1 cup (240ml) red wine (optional)
- 2 cans (14 oz each) crushed tomatoes
- 2 tablespoons tomato paste
- 1 teaspoon dried oregano
- 1 teaspoon dried basil
- 1/2 teaspoon dried thyme
- Salt and black pepper to taste
- 1 cup (240ml) beef or vegetable broth
- 1/2 cup (120ml) whole milk
- 1/4 teaspoon nutmeg (optional)
- 1 pound (450g) spaghetti
- Grated Parmesan cheese for serving
- Fresh basil or parsley for garnish

Instructions:

Heat olive oil in a large pan over medium heat. Add the ground beef and cook until browned, breaking it apart with a spoon as it cooks. Remove any excess fat. Add chopped onions, carrots, celery, and minced garlic to the pan. Sauté until the vegetables are softened.

If using red wine, pour it into the pan and allow it to simmer for a few minutes until it reduces by half.

Add crushed tomatoes, tomato paste, dried oregano, dried basil, dried thyme, salt, and black pepper to the pan. Stir well to combine.

Pour in the beef or vegetable broth and bring the mixture to a simmer. Reduce the heat to low, cover the pan, and let it simmer for at least 1 hour, stirring occasionally. The longer it simmers, the richer the flavor will be.

About 10-15 minutes before serving, add the whole milk and nutmeg to the sauce. Stir well and let it simmer.

While the sauce is simmering, cook the spaghetti according to the package instructions. Drain and set aside.

Taste the Bolognese sauce and adjust the seasoning if needed.

Serve the Bolognese sauce over cooked spaghetti. Garnish with grated Parmesan cheese and fresh basil or parsley.

Enjoy your homemade Spaghetti Bolognese!

Fettuccine Alfredo

Ingredients:

- 1 pound (450g) fettuccine pasta
- 1 cup (240g) unsalted butter
- 1 cup (240ml) heavy cream
- 1 cup (100g) grated Parmesan cheese
- Salt and black pepper to taste
- Fresh parsley, chopped (for garnish)

Instructions:

Cook the fettuccine pasta according to the package instructions in a large pot of salted boiling water. Drain the pasta and set aside.
In a large skillet, melt the butter over medium heat.
Add the heavy cream to the melted butter and bring it to a gentle simmer. Allow it to simmer for 2-3 minutes.
Gradually whisk in the grated Parmesan cheese, stirring continuously to avoid lumps. Continue to cook and stir until the cheese is fully melted and the sauce has thickened.
Season the Alfredo sauce with salt and black pepper to taste. Keep in mind that Parmesan is salty, so adjust accordingly.
Add the cooked fettuccine pasta to the skillet with the Alfredo sauce. Toss the pasta in the sauce until it is well coated.
Cook for an additional 2-3 minutes, allowing the pasta to absorb the flavors of the sauce.
Remove from heat and serve immediately. Garnish with chopped fresh parsley and additional Parmesan cheese if desired.

Enjoy your creamy and delicious Fettuccine Alfredo!

Penne alla Vodka

Ingredients:

- 1 pound (450g) penne pasta
- 2 tablespoons olive oil
- 1 onion, finely chopped
- 3 cloves garlic, minced
- 1/2 teaspoon red pepper flakes (adjust to taste)
- 1 cup (240ml) vodka
- 1 can (28 oz) crushed tomatoes
- 1 cup (240ml) heavy cream
- Salt and black pepper to taste
- 1/2 cup (50g) grated Parmesan cheese
- Fresh basil or parsley, chopped (for garnish)

Instructions:

Cook the penne pasta according to the package instructions in a large pot of salted boiling water. Drain the pasta and set aside.

In a large skillet, heat olive oil over medium heat. Add the chopped onion and sauté until it becomes translucent.

Add minced garlic and red pepper flakes to the skillet. Sauté for an additional minute until the garlic becomes fragrant.

Pour in the vodka and let it simmer for about 3-5 minutes, allowing it to reduce slightly.

Add the crushed tomatoes to the skillet, stirring to combine. Season with salt and black pepper to taste.

Lower the heat to medium-low and simmer the sauce for about 15-20 minutes, allowing the flavors to meld together.

Stir in the heavy cream and continue to simmer for an additional 5-7 minutes until the sauce thickens.

Add the cooked penne pasta to the skillet, tossing to coat the pasta evenly with the sauce.

Mix in the grated Parmesan cheese until it melts and the sauce is creamy.

Remove from heat and garnish with chopped fresh basil or parsley.

Serve your Penne alla Vodka immediately, and enjoy the rich and flavorful dish!

Carbonara

Ingredients:

- 1 pound (450g) spaghetti
- 1 tablespoon olive oil
- 8 ounces (225g) pancetta or guanciale, diced
- 4 large eggs
- 1 cup (100g) grated Pecorino Romano cheese
- 1 cup (100g) grated Parmesan cheese
- 4 cloves garlic, minced
- Salt and black pepper to taste
- Fresh parsley, chopped (for garnish)

Instructions:

Cook the spaghetti according to the package instructions in a large pot of salted boiling water until al dente. Reserve about 1 cup of pasta cooking water before draining.

While the pasta is cooking, heat olive oil in a large skillet over medium heat. Add diced pancetta or guanciale and cook until it becomes crispy.

In a mixing bowl, whisk together the eggs, grated Pecorino Romano, and grated Parmesan cheese. Season with black pepper. Set aside.

Once the pasta is cooked, add it to the skillet with the crispy pancetta. Toss to combine and coat the pasta with the rendered fat from the pancetta.

Remove the skillet from heat and quickly pour the egg and cheese mixture over the pasta, tossing continuously to create a creamy sauce. If the sauce is too thick, add a bit of the reserved pasta cooking water to achieve the desired consistency.

Add minced garlic to the pasta and continue tossing until the garlic is well distributed.

Season with salt and additional black pepper if needed.

Garnish with chopped fresh parsley and serve immediately.

Enjoy your delicious and creamy Carbonara!

Pesto Pasta

Ingredients:

- 1 pound (450g) pasta (spaghetti, linguine, or your favorite type)
- 2 cups (about 60g) fresh basil leaves, packed
- 1/2 cup (120ml) extra-virgin olive oil
- 1/2 cup (60g) grated Parmesan cheese
- 1/3 cup (40g) pine nuts or walnuts
- 3 cloves garlic, peeled
- Salt and black pepper to taste
- Optional: 1 cup (240ml) cherry tomatoes, halved
- Optional: Grated Parmesan cheese for serving

Instructions:

Cook the pasta according to the package instructions in a large pot of salted boiling water. Reserve about 1 cup of pasta cooking water before draining.
In a food processor, combine the fresh basil, pine nuts or walnuts, grated Parmesan, and peeled garlic cloves. Pulse until the ingredients are finely chopped.
With the food processor running, slowly stream in the olive oil until the mixture forms a smooth pesto sauce. You may need to stop and scrape down the sides of the processor with a spatula.
Season the pesto with salt and black pepper to taste. Adjust the consistency by adding a bit of the reserved pasta cooking water if needed.
Toss the cooked pasta with the pesto sauce until it is evenly coated.
If you like, add halved cherry tomatoes to the pasta and toss gently.
Serve the pesto pasta with an additional sprinkle of grated Parmesan cheese if desired.

Enjoy your delicious and fresh Pesto Pasta!

Shrimp Scampi Linguine

Ingredients:

- 1 pound (450g) linguine
- 1 pound (450g) large shrimp, peeled and deveined
- 4 tablespoons unsalted butter
- 4 tablespoons olive oil
- 4 cloves garlic, minced
- 1/2 teaspoon red pepper flakes (adjust to taste)
- 1/2 cup (120ml) dry white wine
- Juice of 1 lemon
- Salt and black pepper to taste
- 1/4 cup (60g) chopped fresh parsley
- Grated Parmesan cheese for serving

Instructions:

Cook the linguine according to the package instructions in a large pot of salted boiling water. Drain and set aside.
In a large skillet, heat 2 tablespoons of butter and 2 tablespoons of olive oil over medium heat.
Add the minced garlic and red pepper flakes to the skillet. Sauté for about 1-2 minutes until the garlic becomes fragrant.
Add the shrimp to the skillet and cook for 2-3 minutes per side until they turn pink and opaque. Season with salt and black pepper.
Remove the shrimp from the skillet and set them aside.
In the same skillet, add the white wine and lemon juice. Bring it to a simmer and let it cook for 2-3 minutes to reduce slightly.
Add the remaining 2 tablespoons of butter and 2 tablespoons of olive oil to the skillet. Stir until the butter is melted.
Toss the cooked linguine into the skillet, coating it with the garlic and lemon-infused sauce.
Add the cooked shrimp back to the skillet, mixing well with the pasta.
Sprinkle chopped fresh parsley over the dish and toss to combine.
Serve the Shrimp Scampi Linguine immediately, garnished with grated Parmesan cheese.

Enjoy your delicious and savory Shrimp Scampi Linguine!

Garlic Butter Pasta

Ingredients:

- 1 pound (450g) pasta (spaghetti, fettuccine, or your choice)
- 1/2 cup (1 stick or 115g) unsalted butter
- 4 cloves garlic, minced
- Red pepper flakes (optional, for a bit of heat)
- Salt and black pepper to taste
- Fresh parsley, chopped (for garnish)
- Grated Parmesan cheese (optional, for serving)

Instructions:

Cook the pasta according to the package instructions in a large pot of salted boiling water. Reserve about 1 cup of pasta cooking water before draining.
While the pasta is cooking, melt the butter in a large skillet over medium heat. Add minced garlic to the melted butter. If you like a bit of heat, you can add red pepper flakes to taste.
Sauté the garlic in the butter until it becomes fragrant and just starts to turn golden, about 2-3 minutes. Be careful not to let it burn.
Drain the cooked pasta and add it to the skillet with the garlic butter.
Toss the pasta in the garlic butter until it is well coated. If the pasta seems too dry, add a bit of the reserved pasta cooking water to achieve your desired consistency.
Season the dish with salt and black pepper to taste.
Garnish with chopped fresh parsley and, if you like, serve with grated Parmesan cheese.
Serve your Garlic Butter Pasta immediately.

Enjoy your quick and flavorful Garlic Butter Pasta!

Chicken Parmesan Pasta

Ingredients:

For the Chicken:

- 1 pound (450g) boneless, skinless chicken breasts
- Salt and black pepper to taste
- 1 cup (120g) all-purpose flour
- 2 large eggs, beaten
- 1 cup (100g) breadcrumbs
- 1/2 cup (50g) grated Parmesan cheese
- 2 tablespoons olive oil

For the Pasta:

- 1 pound (450g) pasta (spaghetti, fettuccine, or your choice)
- 2 cups (480ml) marinara sauce
- 1 cup (100g) shredded mozzarella cheese
- 1/4 cup (25g) grated Parmesan cheese
- Fresh basil or parsley, chopped (for garnish)

Instructions:

Preheat the oven to 375°F (190°C).
Season the chicken breasts with salt and black pepper.
Dredge each chicken breast in flour, dip into beaten eggs, and coat with a mixture of breadcrumbs and grated Parmesan cheese.
Heat olive oil in a skillet over medium-high heat. Cook the breaded chicken breasts for 3-4 minutes per side, or until golden brown and cooked through.
Transfer to a cutting board and let them rest for a few minutes before slicing into strips.
Meanwhile, cook the pasta according to the package instructions in a large pot of salted boiling water. Drain and set aside.
In a baking dish, spread a thin layer of marinara sauce. Place the cooked pasta on top.
Arrange the sliced chicken over the pasta and top with the remaining marinara sauce.
Sprinkle shredded mozzarella and grated Parmesan cheese over the chicken and pasta.

Bake in the preheated oven for about 20-25 minutes, or until the cheese is melted and bubbly.
Garnish with chopped fresh basil or parsley before serving.

Serve your Chicken Parmesan Pasta hot and enjoy this comforting and flavorful meal!

Tomato Basil Pasta

Ingredients:

- 1 pound (450g) pasta (spaghetti, penne, or your choice)
- 3 tablespoons olive oil
- 4 cloves garlic, minced
- 1 can (28 oz) crushed tomatoes
- 1/2 teaspoon red pepper flakes (optional, for a bit of heat)
- Salt and black pepper to taste
- 1 cup (about 25g) fresh basil leaves, chopped
- Grated Parmesan cheese for serving

Instructions:

Cook the pasta according to the package instructions in a large pot of salted boiling water. Reserve about 1 cup of pasta cooking water before draining.
While the pasta is cooking, heat olive oil in a large skillet over medium heat.
Add minced garlic to the olive oil and sauté until it becomes fragrant, about 1-2 minutes. Be careful not to let it brown.
Pour in the crushed tomatoes and red pepper flakes (if using). Season with salt and black pepper to taste.
Simmer the sauce for about 15-20 minutes, allowing it to thicken and the flavors to meld.
Add the chopped fresh basil to the tomato sauce and stir to combine. Let it cook for an additional 2-3 minutes.
Toss the cooked pasta into the skillet with the tomato basil sauce, coating it evenly.
If needed, add a bit of the reserved pasta cooking water to achieve the desired consistency.
Serve your Tomato Basil Pasta hot, garnished with grated Parmesan cheese.

Enjoy this simple and delicious pasta dish with the vibrant flavors of tomato and basil!

Aglio e Olio

Ingredients:

- 1 pound (450g) spaghetti
- 1/2 cup (120ml) extra-virgin olive oil
- 6 cloves garlic, thinly sliced
- 1 teaspoon red pepper flakes (adjust to taste)
- Salt to taste
- Fresh parsley, chopped (for garnish)
- Grated Parmesan cheese (optional, for serving)

Instructions:

Cook the spaghetti according to the package instructions in a large pot of salted boiling water. Reserve about 1 cup of pasta cooking water before draining.
While the pasta is cooking, heat the olive oil in a large skillet over medium heat.
Add thinly sliced garlic to the olive oil and sauté until it turns golden but not browned, about 1-2 minutes. Be cautious not to burn the garlic.
Add red pepper flakes to the skillet, adjusting the quantity according to your spice preference.
Reduce the heat to low, and let the garlic infuse the olive oil for an additional 2-3 minutes.
Once the spaghetti is cooked, transfer it directly from the pot to the skillet using tongs. Toss the pasta to coat it evenly with the garlic-infused oil.
If needed, add a bit of the reserved pasta cooking water to achieve a silky and well-coated consistency.
Season the Aglio e Olio with salt to taste.
Garnish with chopped fresh parsley and, if desired, serve with grated Parmesan cheese.

This dish is best enjoyed immediately, highlighting the simplicity of garlic and olive oil with a hint of red pepper flakes. Enjoy your Aglio e Olio!

Cajun Chicken Pasta

Ingredients:

- 8 oz (225g) linguine or fettuccine
- 2 boneless, skinless chicken breasts, thinly sliced
- Cajun seasoning (store-bought or homemade)
- 2 tablespoons olive oil
- 1 red bell pepper, thinly sliced
- 1 yellow bell pepper, thinly sliced
- 1 onion, thinly sliced
- 3 cloves garlic, minced
- 1 cup (240ml) chicken broth
- 1 cup (240ml) heavy cream
- 1 teaspoon paprika
- Salt and black pepper to taste
- Fresh parsley, chopped (for garnish)
- Grated Parmesan cheese (optional, for serving)

Instructions:

Cook the linguine or fettuccine according to the package instructions in a large pot of salted boiling water. Drain and set aside.

Season the thinly sliced chicken breasts with Cajun seasoning. Adjust the amount according to your spice preference.

Heat olive oil in a large skillet over medium-high heat. Add the seasoned chicken slices and cook until they are browned on both sides and cooked through.

Remove the chicken from the skillet and set aside.

In the same skillet, add sliced red and yellow bell peppers, and onion. Sauté until the vegetables are tender.

Add minced garlic to the vegetables and cook for an additional minute until it becomes fragrant.

Pour in the chicken broth, scraping any browned bits from the bottom of the skillet.

Stir in the heavy cream and paprika. Allow the sauce to simmer and thicken for 3-4 minutes.

Season the sauce with salt and black pepper to taste.

Add the cooked chicken back to the skillet, tossing it in the Cajun-flavored sauce.

Toss the cooked pasta into the skillet, coating it evenly with the creamy Cajun sauce.
Serve the Cajun Chicken Pasta hot, garnished with chopped fresh parsley.
Optionally, sprinkle grated Parmesan cheese on top.

Enjoy your delicious and spicy Cajun Chicken Pasta!

Primavera Pasta

Ingredients:

- 1 pound (450g) fettuccine or your favorite pasta
- 2 tablespoons olive oil
- 1 onion, thinly sliced
- 2 bell peppers (assorted colors), thinly sliced
- 1 zucchini, thinly sliced
- 1 yellow squash, thinly sliced
- 1 cup (150g) cherry tomatoes, halved
- 1 cup (240ml) vegetable broth
- 3 cloves garlic, minced
- 1 teaspoon dried Italian herbs (oregano, thyme, basil)
- Salt and black pepper to taste
- 1/2 cup (120ml) heavy cream or half-and-half
- Grated Parmesan cheese for serving
- Fresh basil or parsley, chopped (for garnish)

Instructions:

Cook the pasta according to the package instructions in a large pot of salted boiling water. Reserve about 1 cup of pasta cooking water before draining.
In a large skillet, heat olive oil over medium heat. Add sliced onions, bell peppers, zucchini, and yellow squash. Sauté until the vegetables are tender but still crisp.
Add cherry tomatoes to the skillet and cook for an additional 2-3 minutes until they soften slightly.
Pour in the vegetable broth, minced garlic, and dried Italian herbs. Simmer for 3-4 minutes.
Season the vegetable mixture with salt and black pepper to taste.
Add heavy cream or half-and-half to the skillet, stirring to combine. Let it simmer for an additional 2-3 minutes.
Toss the cooked pasta into the skillet, coating it evenly with the creamy vegetable sauce. If needed, add a bit of the reserved pasta cooking water to achieve the desired consistency.
Serve the Primavera Pasta hot, garnished with grated Parmesan cheese and chopped fresh basil or parsley.

Enjoy your vibrant and flavorful Primavera Pasta!

Lemon Garlic Shrimp Pasta

Ingredients:

- 1 pound (450g) linguine or spaghetti
- 1 pound (450g) large shrimp, peeled and deveined
- Salt and black pepper to taste
- 3 tablespoons olive oil
- 4 cloves garlic, minced
- Zest of 1 lemon
- Juice of 2 lemons
- 1/2 cup (120ml) chicken broth
- 1/4 teaspoon red pepper flakes (optional, for heat)
- 1/2 cup (120ml) heavy cream
- 1/2 cup (60g) grated Parmesan cheese
- Fresh parsley, chopped (for garnish)

Instructions:

Cook the linguine or spaghetti according to the package instructions in a large pot of salted boiling water. Drain and set aside.

Season the shrimp with salt and black pepper.

In a large skillet, heat olive oil over medium-high heat. Add the seasoned shrimp and cook for 2-3 minutes per side or until they are pink and opaque. Remove the shrimp from the skillet and set aside.

In the same skillet, add minced garlic and cook for about 1 minute until it becomes fragrant.

Add lemon zest, lemon juice, chicken broth, and red pepper flakes (if using). Bring the mixture to a simmer and let it cook for 2-3 minutes.

Reduce the heat to medium-low, stir in the heavy cream, and let it simmer for an additional 2-3 minutes.

Stir in the grated Parmesan cheese, allowing it to melt and create a creamy sauce.

Toss the cooked pasta into the skillet, coating it evenly with the lemon garlic cream sauce.

Add the cooked shrimp back to the skillet, tossing to combine.

Season with additional salt and black pepper if needed.

Serve the Lemon Garlic Shrimp Pasta hot, garnished with chopped fresh parsley.

Enjoy your zesty and flavorful Lemon Garlic Shrimp Pasta!

Mushroom and Spinach Alfredo

Ingredients:

- 1 pound (450g) fettuccine or your favorite pasta
- 2 tablespoons unsalted butter
- 2 tablespoons olive oil
- 8 oz (225g) mushrooms, sliced
- 4 cloves garlic, minced
- 4 cups (about 120g) fresh spinach leaves
- 1 cup (240ml) heavy cream
- 1 cup (100g) grated Parmesan cheese
- Salt and black pepper to taste
- Pinch of nutmeg (optional)
- Fresh parsley, chopped (for garnish)

Instructions:

Cook the pasta according to the package instructions in a large pot of salted boiling water. Reserve about 1 cup of pasta cooking water before draining.
In a large skillet, melt butter and olive oil over medium heat.
Add sliced mushrooms to the skillet and sauté until they are browned and cooked through.
Add minced garlic to the mushrooms and cook for an additional 1-2 minutes until it becomes fragrant.
Add fresh spinach to the skillet, stirring until wilted.
Pour in the heavy cream, stirring to combine. Let it simmer for 2-3 minutes.
Stir in the grated Parmesan cheese until the sauce is smooth and creamy.
Season the Alfredo sauce with salt, black pepper, and a pinch of nutmeg if using.
Toss the cooked pasta into the skillet, coating it evenly with the mushroom and spinach Alfredo sauce. If needed, add a bit of the reserved pasta cooking water to achieve the desired consistency.
Serve the Mushroom and Spinach Alfredo hot, garnished with chopped fresh parsley.

Enjoy your creamy and flavorful Mushroom and Spinach Alfredo pasta!

Baked Ziti

Ingredients:

- 1 pound (450g) ziti or penne pasta
- 1 pound (450g) ground Italian sausage or ground beef
- 1 onion, finely chopped
- 3 cloves garlic, minced
- 1 can (28 oz) crushed tomatoes
- 1 can (15 oz) tomato sauce
- 1 teaspoon dried oregano
- 1 teaspoon dried basil
- Salt and black pepper to taste
- 2 cups (480ml) ricotta cheese
- 1 large egg
- 3 cups (300g) shredded mozzarella cheese
- 1 cup (100g) grated Parmesan cheese
- Fresh basil or parsley, chopped (for garnish)

Instructions:

Preheat your oven to 375°F (190°C).

Cook the ziti or penne pasta according to the package instructions in a large pot of salted boiling water. Drain and set aside.

In a large skillet, cook the ground Italian sausage or beef over medium-high heat until browned. Add chopped onion and minced garlic, and cook until the onion is softened.

Add crushed tomatoes, tomato sauce, dried oregano, dried basil, salt, and black pepper to the skillet. Simmer the sauce for about 10-15 minutes, allowing the flavors to meld.

In a bowl, combine ricotta cheese and the egg. Mix well.

In a large mixing bowl, combine the cooked pasta with the meat sauce. Stir until the pasta is well coated.

In a 9x13-inch baking dish, layer half of the pasta mixture. Spoon half of the ricotta mixture over the pasta, and sprinkle with half of the mozzarella and Parmesan cheeses.

Repeat the layering process with the remaining pasta, ricotta mixture, and cheeses.

Cover the baking dish with aluminum foil and bake in the preheated oven for 25 minutes.
Remove the foil and bake for an additional 10-15 minutes, or until the cheese is bubbly and golden.
Let the Baked Ziti rest for a few minutes before serving.
Garnish with chopped fresh basil or parsley before serving.

Enjoy your delicious and comforting Baked Ziti!

Pasta Puttanesca

Ingredients:

- 1 pound (450g) spaghetti or linguine
- 3 tablespoons olive oil
- 4 cloves garlic, minced
- 6 anchovy fillets, chopped
- 1/2 teaspoon red pepper flakes (adjust to taste)
- 1 can (28 oz) crushed tomatoes
- 1/2 cup (120g) pitted Kalamata olives, sliced
- 2 tablespoons capers, drained
- 2 tablespoons chopped fresh parsley
- Salt and black pepper to taste
- Grated Parmesan cheese for serving

Instructions:

Cook the pasta according to the package instructions in a large pot of salted boiling water. Reserve about 1 cup of pasta cooking water before draining.
In a large skillet, heat olive oil over medium heat. Add minced garlic, chopped anchovy fillets, and red pepper flakes. Sauté for about 2 minutes until the anchovies dissolve into the oil and the garlic is fragrant.
Add crushed tomatoes to the skillet, stirring to combine. Simmer the sauce for about 15-20 minutes, allowing it to thicken.
Stir in sliced olives, drained capers, and chopped fresh parsley. Season with salt and black pepper to taste. Be cautious with the salt as anchovies, olives, and capers are already salty.
If the sauce is too thick, you can add a bit of the reserved pasta cooking water to achieve the desired consistency.
Toss the cooked pasta into the skillet, coating it evenly with the Puttanesca sauce.
Serve the Pasta Puttanesca hot, garnished with grated Parmesan cheese.

Enjoy your bold and flavorful Pasta Puttanesca!

Chicken Piccata Pasta

Ingredients:

For the Chicken:

- 4 boneless, skinless chicken breasts
- Salt and black pepper to taste
- 1 cup (120g) all-purpose flour, for dredging
- 4 tablespoons unsalted butter
- 2 tablespoons olive oil

For the Piccata Sauce:

- 1/2 cup (120ml) chicken broth
- Juice of 2 lemons
- 1/4 cup (60ml) capers, drained
- 1/4 cup (60ml) dry white wine (optional)
- 2 tablespoons chopped fresh parsley

For the Pasta:

- 1 pound (450g) linguine or fettuccine
- Grated Parmesan cheese for serving

Instructions:

Season the chicken breasts with salt and black pepper.
Dredge each chicken breast in flour, shaking off excess.
In a large skillet, heat 2 tablespoons of butter and 1 tablespoon of olive oil over medium-high heat. Add the chicken breasts and cook for 3-4 minutes per side, or until golden brown and cooked through. Remove the chicken from the skillet and set aside.
In the same skillet, add the remaining 2 tablespoons of butter and 1 tablespoon of olive oil.
Add chicken broth, lemon juice, capers, and white wine (if using). Bring the mixture to a simmer, scraping up any browned bits from the bottom of the skillet.
Return the cooked chicken to the skillet, allowing it to heat through in the sauce. Sprinkle chopped fresh parsley over the chicken.
While the chicken is heating in the sauce, cook the pasta according to the package instructions in a large pot of salted boiling water. Drain and set aside.

Toss the cooked pasta in the skillet with the chicken and piccata sauce, coating the pasta evenly.
Serve the Chicken Piccata Pasta hot, garnished with grated Parmesan cheese.

Enjoy this flavorful and elegant Chicken Piccata Pasta!

Beef Stroganoff Pasta

Ingredients:

- 1 pound (450g) fettuccine or egg noodles
- 1.5 pounds (680g) beef sirloin or tenderloin, thinly sliced into strips
- Salt and black pepper to taste
- 2 tablespoons olive oil
- 1 onion, finely chopped
- 2 cloves garlic, minced
- 8 oz (225g) mushrooms, sliced
- 2 tablespoons all-purpose flour
- 1 cup (240ml) beef broth
- 2 tablespoons Worcestershire sauce
- 1 tablespoon Dijon mustard
- 1 cup (240ml) sour cream
- Chopped fresh parsley (for garnish)

Instructions:

Cook the fettuccine or egg noodles according to the package instructions in a large pot of salted boiling water. Drain and set aside.
Season the beef strips with salt and black pepper.
In a large skillet, heat olive oil over medium-high heat. Add the sliced beef and cook until browned on all sides. Remove the beef from the skillet and set aside.
In the same skillet, add chopped onion and cook until softened.
Add minced garlic and sliced mushrooms to the skillet. Sauté until the mushrooms are browned.
Sprinkle flour over the mushroom mixture, stirring constantly for about 1-2 minutes to cook out the raw taste of the flour.
Slowly add beef broth, Worcestershire sauce, and Dijon mustard to the skillet, stirring continuously until the sauce thickens.
Lower the heat to medium-low and stir in sour cream until the sauce is smooth.
Return the cooked beef to the skillet, allowing it to heat through in the sauce.
Adjust seasoning if necessary.
Serve the Beef Stroganoff over the cooked pasta, garnished with chopped fresh parsley.

Enjoy your delicious and creamy Beef Stroganoff Pasta!

One-Pot Creamy Tuscan Chicken Pasta

Ingredients:

- 1 pound (450g) boneless, skinless chicken breasts, cut into bite-sized pieces
- Salt and black pepper to taste
- 2 tablespoons olive oil
- 4 cloves garlic, minced
- 1 teaspoon dried Italian herbs (oregano, thyme, basil)
- 1/2 cup (120ml) chicken broth
- 1 cup (240ml) heavy cream
- 1 cup (100g) grated Parmesan cheese
- 8 oz (225g) sun-dried tomatoes, drained and sliced
- 3 cups (about 90g) fresh baby spinach leaves
- 1 pound (450g) fettuccine or your favorite pasta
- Fresh basil, chopped (for garnish)

Instructions:

Season the chicken pieces with salt and black pepper.
In a large pot or Dutch oven, heat olive oil over medium-high heat. Add the chicken and cook until browned on all sides. Remove the chicken from the pot and set aside.
In the same pot, add minced garlic and dried Italian herbs. Sauté for about 1 minute until the garlic becomes fragrant.
Pour in chicken broth, scraping up any browned bits from the bottom of the pot.
Add heavy cream and grated Parmesan cheese to the pot, stirring until the cheese is melted and the sauce is smooth.
Stir in sliced sun-dried tomatoes.
Return the cooked chicken to the pot and add fresh baby spinach. Cook until the spinach wilts and the chicken is cooked through.
Meanwhile, cook the pasta according to the package instructions in a separate pot of salted boiling water. Drain and set aside.
Toss the cooked pasta into the creamy Tuscan chicken mixture, ensuring it's well coated with the sauce.
Serve the One-Pot Creamy Tuscan Chicken Pasta hot, garnished with chopped fresh basil.

Enjoy your convenient and delicious one-pot meal!

Broccoli Pesto Pasta

Ingredients:

- 1 pound (450g) pasta (spaghetti, fettuccine, or your choice)
- 4 cups (about 400g) broccoli florets
- 1/2 cup (60g) grated Parmesan cheese
- 1/2 cup (120ml) extra-virgin olive oil
- 1/3 cup (40g) pine nuts or walnuts
- 3 cloves garlic, peeled
- Juice of 1 lemon
- Salt and black pepper to taste
- Red pepper flakes (optional, for a bit of heat)
- Grated Pecorino Romano cheese for serving (optional)

Instructions:

Cook the pasta according to the package instructions in a large pot of salted boiling water. Reserve about 1 cup of pasta cooking water before draining.
While the pasta is cooking, blanch the broccoli florets in boiling water for about 2-3 minutes or until they are bright green and slightly tender. Drain and set aside.
In a food processor, combine the blanched broccoli, grated Parmesan, olive oil, pine nuts or walnuts, peeled garlic cloves, and lemon juice. Pulse until you achieve a smooth pesto-like consistency.
Season the broccoli pesto with salt and black pepper to taste. Add red pepper flakes if you want a bit of heat.
Toss the cooked pasta with the broccoli pesto, ensuring it is well coated. If needed, add a bit of the reserved pasta cooking water to adjust the consistency.
Serve the Broccoli Pesto Pasta hot, optionally garnished with grated Pecorino Romano cheese.

Enjoy your nutritious and flavorful Broccoli Pesto Pasta!

Caprese Pasta Salad

Ingredients:

- 1 pound (450g) pasta (penne, fusilli, or your choice)
- 2 cups cherry tomatoes, halved
- 8 oz (225g) fresh mozzarella balls (bocconcini), halved
- 1/2 cup fresh basil leaves, chopped
- 1/4 cup (60ml) extra-virgin olive oil
- 2 tablespoons balsamic vinegar
- Salt and black pepper to taste
- 1 teaspoon dried oregano (optional)
- Grated Parmesan cheese for serving (optional)

Instructions:

Cook the pasta according to the package instructions in a large pot of salted boiling water. Drain and let it cool to room temperature.
In a large bowl, combine the cooked pasta, cherry tomatoes, fresh mozzarella, and chopped basil.
In a small bowl, whisk together the olive oil, balsamic vinegar, salt, black pepper, and dried oregano (if using).
Pour the dressing over the pasta salad and toss gently to coat all the ingredients evenly.
Taste and adjust the seasoning if necessary.
Refrigerate the Caprese Pasta Salad for at least 30 minutes to allow the flavors to meld.
Before serving, give the salad a final gentle toss.
Optionally, garnish with grated Parmesan cheese just before serving.

Enjoy your light and flavorful Caprese Pasta Salad!

Goulash

Ingredients:

- 2 pounds (900g) beef stew meat, cut into cubes
- Salt and black pepper to taste
- 3 tablespoons vegetable oil
- 2 large onions, finely chopped
- 3 cloves garlic, minced
- 2 tablespoons sweet paprika
- 1 teaspoon caraway seeds
- 1 tablespoon tomato paste
- 1 red bell pepper, diced
- 1 green bell pepper, diced
- 2 large carrots, peeled and sliced
- 1 can (14 oz) diced tomatoes
- 3 cups (720ml) beef broth
- 2 bay leaves
- 1 tablespoon Worcestershire sauce
- 1 cup (240ml) sour cream (optional, for serving)
- Chopped fresh parsley, for garnish
- Cooked noodles or rice, for serving

Instructions:

Season the beef cubes with salt and black pepper.
In a large Dutch oven or heavy pot, heat the vegetable oil over medium-high heat. Brown the beef in batches, ensuring each side is well-seared. Remove the beef and set aside.
In the same pot, add chopped onions and sauté until they become translucent.
Add minced garlic, sweet paprika, caraway seeds, and tomato paste to the pot. Stir well to coat the onions.
Return the browned beef to the pot. Add diced red and green bell peppers, sliced carrots, diced tomatoes, beef broth, bay leaves, and Worcestershire sauce. Stir to combine.
Bring the mixture to a boil, then reduce the heat to low, cover the pot, and let it simmer for 2-2.5 hours or until the beef is tender.
Adjust the seasoning with salt and black pepper to taste.

If the goulash is too thick, you can add more beef broth or water to reach your desired consistency.
Serve the Beef Goulash hot over cooked noodles or rice.
Optionally, garnish with a dollop of sour cream and chopped fresh parsley.

Enjoy your hearty and flavorful Beef Goulash!

Mediterranean Pasta

Ingredients:

- 1 pound (450g) pasta (penne, fusilli, or your choice)
- 3 tablespoons extra-virgin olive oil
- 4 cloves garlic, minced
- 1 can (14 oz) diced tomatoes, drained
- 1/2 cup Kalamata olives, pitted and sliced
- 1/4 cup capers, drained
- 1 teaspoon dried oregano
- 1 teaspoon dried basil
- Salt and black pepper to taste
- Red pepper flakes (optional, for a bit of heat)
- Feta cheese, crumbled, for serving
- Fresh parsley, chopped, for garnish

Instructions:

Cook the pasta according to the package instructions in a large pot of salted boiling water. Reserve about 1 cup of pasta cooking water before draining.
In a large skillet, heat olive oil over medium heat. Add minced garlic and sauté for about 1-2 minutes until it becomes fragrant.
Add diced tomatoes, Kalamata olives, capers, dried oregano, and dried basil to the skillet. Season with salt, black pepper, and red pepper flakes (if using).
Simmer the sauce for about 5-7 minutes, allowing the flavors to meld.
Toss the cooked pasta into the skillet with the Mediterranean sauce, ensuring it is well coated. If needed, add a bit of the reserved pasta cooking water to achieve the desired consistency.
Serve the Mediterranean Pasta hot, garnished with crumbled feta cheese and chopped fresh parsley.

Enjoy your light and flavorful Mediterranean Pasta! Feel free to customize it with additional ingredients like cherry tomatoes, artichoke hearts, or grilled chicken if you like.

Shrimp and Broccoli Alfredo

Ingredients:

- 1 pound (450g) fettuccine or your favorite pasta
- 1 pound (450g) large shrimp, peeled and deveined
- Salt and black pepper to taste
- 2 tablespoons olive oil
- 4 cloves garlic, minced
- 1 cup (240ml) chicken broth
- 1 cup (240ml) heavy cream
- 1 cup (100g) grated Parmesan cheese
- 2 cups (about 200g) broccoli florets, blanched
- Fresh parsley, chopped (for garnish)

Instructions:

Cook the pasta according to the package instructions in a large pot of salted boiling water. Drain and set aside.
Season the shrimp with salt and black pepper.
In a large skillet, heat olive oil over medium-high heat. Add the seasoned shrimp and cook for 2-3 minutes per side or until they are pink and opaque. Remove the shrimp from the skillet and set aside.
In the same skillet, add minced garlic and sauté for about 1 minute until it becomes fragrant.
Pour in chicken broth, scraping up any browned bits from the bottom of the skillet.
Stir in heavy cream and grated Parmesan cheese. Allow the sauce to simmer for 3-4 minutes, stirring until the cheese is melted and the sauce is smooth.
Add blanched broccoli to the Alfredo sauce and toss to combine.
Return the cooked shrimp to the skillet, allowing them to heat through in the sauce.
Toss the cooked pasta into the skillet, coating it evenly with the Shrimp and Broccoli Alfredo sauce.
Season with additional salt and black pepper if needed.
Serve the Shrimp and Broccoli Alfredo hot, garnished with chopped fresh parsley.

Enjoy your creamy and flavorful Shrimp and Broccoli Alfredo!

Chili Mac

Ingredients:

- 1 pound (450g) elbow macaroni or your favorite pasta
- 1 pound (450g) ground beef
- 1 onion, finely chopped
- 3 cloves garlic, minced
- 1 can (15 oz) kidney beans, drained and rinsed
- 1 can (14 oz) diced tomatoes
- 1 can (6 oz) tomato paste
- 2 cups (480ml) beef broth
- 2 tablespoons chili powder
- 1 teaspoon cumin
- 1 teaspoon paprika
- 1/2 teaspoon oregano
- Salt and black pepper to taste
- Shredded cheddar cheese, for topping
- Sour cream, for serving
- Chopped green onions or fresh cilantro, for garnish

Instructions:

Cook the pasta according to the package instructions in a large pot of salted boiling water. Drain and set aside.

In a large skillet or Dutch oven, brown the ground beef over medium-high heat. Drain any excess fat.

Add chopped onion and minced garlic to the skillet, sautéing until the onion is softened.

Stir in kidney beans, diced tomatoes, tomato paste, beef broth, chili powder, cumin, paprika, oregano, salt, and black pepper. Mix well.

Simmer the chili for about 15-20 minutes, allowing the flavors to meld and the sauce to thicken.

Toss the cooked pasta into the chili, ensuring it's well coated with the sauce.

Serve the Chili Mac hot, topped with shredded cheddar cheese, a dollop of sour cream, and garnished with chopped green onions or fresh cilantro.

Enjoy your hearty and comforting Chili Mac!

Creamy Sun-Dried Tomato Pasta

Ingredients:

- 1 pound (450g) fettuccine or your favorite pasta
- 1 cup (about 100g) sun-dried tomatoes (packed in oil), drained and chopped
- 2 tablespoons olive oil (from the sun-dried tomatoes)
- 4 cloves garlic, minced
- 1 cup (240ml) chicken or vegetable broth
- 1 cup (240ml) heavy cream
- 1/2 cup (50g) grated Parmesan cheese
- Salt and black pepper to taste
- Crushed red pepper flakes (optional, for heat)
- Fresh basil, chopped (for garnish)

Instructions:

Cook the pasta according to the package instructions in a large pot of salted boiling water. Reserve about 1 cup of pasta cooking water before draining.
In a large skillet, heat the olive oil from the sun-dried tomatoes over medium heat. Add minced garlic and sauté for about 1-2 minutes until it becomes fragrant.
Add chopped sun-dried tomatoes to the skillet and sauté for an additional 2-3 minutes.
Pour in chicken or vegetable broth, stirring to deglaze the pan.
Stir in heavy cream, grated Parmesan cheese, salt, black pepper, and crushed red pepper flakes (if using). Simmer the sauce for 3-4 minutes until it thickens.
Toss the cooked pasta into the skillet, coating it evenly with the creamy sun-dried tomato sauce. If needed, add a bit of the reserved pasta cooking water to achieve the desired consistency.
Serve the Creamy Sun-Dried Tomato Pasta hot, garnished with chopped fresh basil.

Enjoy your luscious and flavorful Creamy Sun-Dried Tomato Pasta!

Sausage and Peppers Pasta

Ingredients:

- 1 pound (450g) pasta (penne, rigatoni, or your choice)
- 1 pound (450g) Italian sausage, casings removed
- 2 tablespoons olive oil
- 1 onion, thinly sliced
- 2 bell peppers (assorted colors), sliced
- 3 cloves garlic, minced
- 1 can (14 oz) crushed tomatoes
- 1 teaspoon dried oregano
- 1 teaspoon dried basil
- Salt and black pepper to taste
- Red pepper flakes (optional, for heat)
- Fresh parsley, chopped (for garnish)
- Grated Parmesan cheese for serving

Instructions:

Cook the pasta according to the package instructions in a large pot of salted boiling water. Reserve about 1 cup of pasta cooking water before draining.

In a large skillet, heat olive oil over medium-high heat. Add the Italian sausage, breaking it apart with a spatula as it cooks. Cook until browned and cooked through. Remove excess fat if needed.

Add sliced onions and bell peppers to the skillet. Sauté until the vegetables are softened.

Add minced garlic and continue to sauté for an additional 1-2 minutes until fragrant.

Pour in crushed tomatoes, dried oregano, dried basil, salt, black pepper, and red pepper flakes (if using). Stir well to combine.

Simmer the sauce for about 10-15 minutes, allowing the flavors to meld and the sauce to thicken.

Toss the cooked pasta into the skillet, coating it evenly with the sausage and peppers sauce. If needed, add a bit of the reserved pasta cooking water to achieve the desired consistency.

Serve the Sausage and Peppers Pasta hot, garnished with chopped fresh parsley and grated Parmesan cheese.

Enjoy your hearty and flavorful Sausage and Peppers Pasta!

Lobster Ravioli

Ingredients:

For the Lobster Ravioli:

- 1 package (about 12-16 pieces) lobster ravioli (store-bought or homemade)
- Salted water for boiling

For the Sauce:

- 2 tablespoons unsalted butter
- 2 tablespoons olive oil
- 4 cloves garlic, minced
- 1/2 cup (120ml) heavy cream
- 1/2 cup (120ml) chicken or seafood broth
- 1/4 cup (60ml) dry white wine (optional)
- Salt and black pepper to taste
- Fresh parsley, chopped (for garnish)
- Grated Parmesan cheese (for serving)

Instructions:

Bring a large pot of salted water to a boil. Cook the lobster ravioli according to the package instructions or until they float to the surface (if homemade). Drain and set aside.
In a large skillet, heat butter and olive oil over medium heat.
Add minced garlic to the skillet and sauté for about 1-2 minutes until it becomes fragrant.
Pour in heavy cream, chicken or seafood broth, and white wine (if using). Stir well and let it simmer for 3-4 minutes, allowing the sauce to thicken.
Season the sauce with salt and black pepper to taste.
Add the cooked lobster ravioli to the skillet, tossing gently to coat them with the sauce.
Serve the Lobster Ravioli hot, garnished with chopped fresh parsley and grated Parmesan cheese.

Enjoy your decadent and flavorful Lobster Ravioli!

Pasta e Fagioli

Ingredients:

- 2 tablespoons olive oil
- 1 onion, finely chopped
- 2 carrots, diced
- 2 celery stalks, diced
- 4 cloves garlic, minced
- 1 can (15 oz) cannellini beans, drained and rinsed
- 1 can (15 oz) red kidney beans, drained and rinsed
- 1 can (14 oz) diced tomatoes
- 4 cups (960ml) vegetable or chicken broth
- 1 teaspoon dried oregano
- 1 teaspoon dried basil
- 1/2 teaspoon dried thyme
- Salt and black pepper to taste
- 1 cup (200g) ditalini or small pasta of your choice
- Fresh parsley, chopped (for garnish)
- Grated Parmesan cheese (for serving)

Instructions:

In a large pot, heat olive oil over medium heat. Add chopped onion, carrots, and celery. Sauté until the vegetables are softened.
Add minced garlic and continue to sauté for an additional 1-2 minutes until fragrant.
Pour in diced tomatoes, cannellini beans, red kidney beans, vegetable or chicken broth, dried oregano, dried basil, dried thyme, salt, and black pepper. Stir well to combine.
Bring the soup to a boil, then reduce the heat to low and let it simmer for about 15-20 minutes.
Meanwhile, cook the pasta in a separate pot according to the package instructions. Drain and set aside.
Add the cooked pasta to the soup and stir to combine. Let it simmer for an additional 5-7 minutes until the pasta is heated through.
Adjust the seasoning with salt and black pepper if necessary.
Serve Pasta e Fagioli hot, garnished with chopped fresh parsley and grated Parmesan cheese.

Enjoy your comforting and delicious Pasta e Fagioli soup!

Thai Peanut Noodles

Ingredients:

For the Peanut Sauce:

- 1/2 cup (120g) peanut butter
- 3 tablespoons soy sauce
- 2 tablespoons rice vinegar
- 2 tablespoons sesame oil
- 1 tablespoon honey or maple syrup
- 1 teaspoon grated ginger
- 2 cloves garlic, minced
- 1/2 teaspoon red pepper flakes (adjust to taste)
- 1/4 cup (60ml) warm water (to thin the sauce)

For the Noodles:

- 8 oz (225g) rice noodles or your favorite noodles
- 2 tablespoons vegetable oil
- 1 red bell pepper, julienned
- 1 carrot, julienned or shredded
- 1 cup (150g) broccoli florets, blanched
- 1 cup (100g) bean sprouts
- 2 green onions, sliced
- Crushed peanuts and fresh cilantro (for garnish)

Instructions:

Cook the noodles according to the package instructions in a large pot of salted boiling water. Drain and set aside.

In a bowl, whisk together all the ingredients for the peanut sauce until well combined. If the sauce is too thick, add warm water a little at a time until it reaches your desired consistency.

In a large skillet or wok, heat vegetable oil over medium-high heat. Add julienned red bell pepper, julienned or shredded carrot, and blanched broccoli florets. Stir-fry for about 3-4 minutes until the vegetables are tender-crisp.

Add the cooked noodles to the skillet and pour the peanut sauce over them. Toss everything together to coat the noodles and vegetables evenly.

Add bean sprouts and sliced green onions, tossing for an additional 1-2 minutes until the bean sprouts are just wilted.
Remove from heat and garnish with crushed peanuts and fresh cilantro.
Serve Thai Peanut Noodles warm or at room temperature.

Enjoy your flavorful and satisfying Thai Peanut Noodles!

Spinach and Artichoke Pasta

Ingredients:

- 8 oz (225g) penne or your favorite pasta
- 2 tablespoons olive oil
- 1 small onion, finely chopped
- 3 cloves garlic, minced
- 1 can (14 oz) artichoke hearts, drained and chopped
- 4 cups fresh baby spinach leaves
- 1 cup (240ml) vegetable or chicken broth
- 1 cup (240ml) heavy cream
- 1 cup (100g) grated Parmesan cheese
- Salt and black pepper to taste
- Red pepper flakes (optional, for heat)
- 1/2 cup (60g) shredded mozzarella cheese
- Fresh parsley, chopped (for garnish)

Instructions:

Cook the pasta according to the package instructions in a large pot of salted boiling water. Drain and set aside.

In a large skillet, heat olive oil over medium heat. Add chopped onion and sauté until it becomes translucent.

Add minced garlic to the skillet and sauté for about 1 minute until fragrant.

Stir in chopped artichoke hearts and fresh baby spinach. Cook until the spinach wilts.

Pour in vegetable or chicken broth, heavy cream, and grated Parmesan cheese. Stir well to combine.

Season the sauce with salt, black pepper, and red pepper flakes (if using).

Simmer the sauce for 3-4 minutes until it thickens.

Toss the cooked pasta into the skillet, coating it evenly with the spinach and artichoke sauce.

Transfer the pasta to an oven-safe dish and sprinkle shredded mozzarella cheese on top.

Broil in the oven for 2-3 minutes or until the cheese is melted and bubbly.

Garnish the Spinach and Artichoke Pasta with chopped fresh parsley.

Serve your creamy and flavorful Spinach and Artichoke Pasta warm. Enjoy!

Chicken and Mushroom Fettuccine

Ingredients:

- 8 oz (225g) fettuccine pasta
- 1 pound (450g) boneless, skinless chicken breasts, cut into bite-sized pieces
- Salt and black pepper to taste
- 2 tablespoons olive oil
- 8 oz (225g) cremini or white mushrooms, sliced
- 4 cloves garlic, minced
- 1 cup (240ml) chicken broth
- 1 cup (240ml) heavy cream
- 1 cup (100g) grated Parmesan cheese
- 2 tablespoons unsalted butter
- 1 teaspoon dried thyme
- Chopped fresh parsley (for garnish)

Instructions:

Cook the fettuccine pasta according to the package instructions in a large pot of salted boiling water. Drain and set aside.
Season the chicken pieces with salt and black pepper.
In a large skillet, heat olive oil over medium-high heat. Add the seasoned chicken and cook until browned on all sides and cooked through. Remove the chicken from the skillet and set aside.
In the same skillet, add sliced mushrooms and sauté until they release their moisture and become golden brown.
Add minced garlic to the skillet and sauté for about 1 minute until it becomes fragrant.
Pour in chicken broth, heavy cream, grated Parmesan cheese, unsalted butter, and dried thyme. Stir well to combine.
Allow the sauce to simmer for 3-4 minutes, stirring until the cheese is melted and the sauce is smooth.
Return the cooked chicken to the skillet, allowing it to heat through in the sauce.
Toss the cooked fettuccine into the skillet, coating it evenly with the Chicken and Mushroom Alfredo sauce.
Adjust the seasoning if necessary and serve the Chicken and Mushroom Fettuccine hot, garnished with chopped fresh parsley.

Enjoy your creamy and indulgent Chicken and Mushroom Fettuccine!

Butternut Squash Ravioli

Ingredients:

For the Butternut Squash Filling:

- 1 small butternut squash, peeled, seeded, and diced
- 2 tablespoons olive oil
- Salt and black pepper to taste
- 1/2 teaspoon ground cinnamon
- 1/4 teaspoon ground nutmeg
- 1/4 cup (30g) grated Parmesan cheese
- 1/4 cup (60g) ricotta cheese

For the Pasta Dough:

- 2 cups (250g) all-purpose flour
- 3 large eggs
- 1/2 teaspoon salt

For the Sage Brown Butter Sauce:

- 1/2 cup (115g) unsalted butter
- Fresh sage leaves
- Salt and black pepper to taste
- Grated Parmesan cheese (for serving)

Instructions:

Preheat the oven to 400°F (200°C).
Toss the diced butternut squash with olive oil, salt, black pepper, ground cinnamon, and ground nutmeg. Roast in the preheated oven for about 25-30 minutes or until the squash is tender and slightly caramelized.
In a food processor, combine the roasted butternut squash, grated Parmesan cheese, and ricotta cheese. Blend until smooth. Adjust seasoning if necessary.
For the pasta dough, make a well with the flour on a clean surface. Crack the eggs into the well, add salt, and gradually incorporate the flour into the eggs until a dough forms. Knead the dough for about 8-10 minutes until it becomes smooth. Wrap it in plastic wrap and let it rest for 30 minutes.

Roll out the pasta dough into thin sheets. Place spoonfuls of the butternut squash filling on one sheet, leaving space between each mound.

Lay a second sheet of pasta over the filling and press around each mound to seal the ravioli. Cut the ravioli into individual pieces.

Bring a large pot of salted water to a boil. Cook the ravioli for 3-4 minutes or until they float to the surface. Remove with a slotted spoon and set aside.

For the Sage Brown Butter Sauce, melt unsalted butter in a skillet over medium heat. Add fresh sage leaves and cook until the butter turns a golden brown color. Season with salt and black pepper.

Toss the cooked butternut squash ravioli in the sage brown butter sauce.

Serve the Butternut Squash Ravioli hot, garnished with grated Parmesan cheese.

Enjoy your homemade Butternut Squash Ravioli with Sage Brown Butter Sauce!

Lemon Ricotta Pasta

Ingredients:

- 8 oz (225g) pasta (spaghetti, fettuccine, or your choice)
- 1 cup (240g) ricotta cheese
- Zest of 1 lemon
- Juice of 1 lemon
- 2 tablespoons extra-virgin olive oil
- 2 cloves garlic, minced
- Salt and black pepper to taste
- Red pepper flakes (optional, for heat)
- Fresh basil or parsley, chopped (for garnish)
- Grated Parmesan cheese (for serving)

Instructions:

Cook the pasta according to the package instructions in a large pot of salted boiling water. Reserve about 1 cup of pasta cooking water before draining.
In a large bowl, whisk together ricotta cheese, lemon zest, and lemon juice until well combined.
In a skillet, heat extra-virgin olive oil over medium heat. Add minced garlic and sauté for about 1-2 minutes until fragrant.
Transfer the cooked pasta to the skillet, tossing it with the garlic-infused olive oil. Pour the lemon ricotta mixture over the pasta and toss to coat evenly. If needed, add a bit of the reserved pasta cooking water to achieve the desired consistency.
Season with salt, black pepper, and red pepper flakes (if using). Continue to toss until the pasta is well coated.
Serve the Lemon Ricotta Pasta hot, garnished with chopped fresh basil or parsley, and grated Parmesan cheese.

Enjoy your light and flavorful Lemon Ricotta Pasta!

Cacio e Pepe

Ingredients:

- 8 oz (225g) spaghetti or other pasta of your choice
- 1 cup (100g) Pecorino Romano cheese, finely grated
- 1 tablespoon black pepper, freshly ground
- Salt to taste

Instructions:

Cook the pasta in a large pot of salted boiling water until al dente. Follow the package instructions, and reserve about 1 cup of pasta cooking water before draining.
In a skillet over medium heat, add the freshly ground black pepper. Toast the pepper for about 1-2 minutes, stirring constantly, until it becomes fragrant.
Add a ladle of the reserved pasta cooking water to the skillet with the toasted black pepper and mix well.
Add the cooked pasta to the skillet, tossing it with the pepper-infused water.
Gradually add the finely grated Pecorino Romano cheese to the pasta, tossing continuously to create a creamy sauce. If needed, add more pasta cooking water to achieve the desired consistency.
Continue tossing until the cheese is melted, and the sauce coats the pasta evenly.
Season with salt to taste. Be mindful of the salt because Pecorino Romano is already salty.
Serve Cacio e Pepe immediately, garnished with an extra sprinkle of Pecorino Romano and black pepper.

Enjoy the simplicity and bold flavors of this classic Roman dish, Cacio e Pepe!

Taco Pasta

Ingredients:

- 8 oz (225g) pasta (penne, rotini, or your choice)
- 1 pound (450g) ground beef or turkey
- 1 small onion, finely chopped
- 1 packet (1 oz) taco seasoning mix
- 1 can (14 oz) diced tomatoes, undrained
- 1 can (15 oz) black beans, drained and rinsed
- 1 cup frozen corn kernels
- 1 cup shredded cheddar cheese
- Sour cream, chopped green onions, and chopped fresh cilantro (for garnish)

Instructions:

Cook the pasta according to the package instructions in a large pot of salted boiling water. Drain and set aside.

In a large skillet over medium heat, brown the ground beef or turkey. Drain any excess fat.

Add chopped onion to the skillet and sauté until it becomes translucent.

Stir in the taco seasoning mix, diced tomatoes (with their juice), black beans, and frozen corn. Mix well and let it simmer for about 5-7 minutes.

Add the cooked pasta to the skillet, tossing to coat it evenly with the taco mixture.

Sprinkle shredded cheddar cheese over the pasta and cover the skillet with a lid. Let it sit for a few minutes until the cheese is melted.

Serve the Taco Pasta hot, garnished with dollops of sour cream, chopped green onions, and chopped fresh cilantro.

Enjoy your Taco Pasta, a quick and satisfying twist on traditional tacos!

Shrimp Fra Diavolo

Ingredients:

- 8 oz (225g) linguine or your favorite pasta
- 1 pound (450g) large shrimp, peeled and deveined
- Salt and black pepper to taste
- 3 tablespoons olive oil
- 4 cloves garlic, minced
- 1/2 teaspoon red pepper flakes (adjust to taste)
- 1 can (14 oz) crushed tomatoes
- 1/2 cup (120ml) dry white wine
- 1 teaspoon dried oregano
- 1 teaspoon dried basil
- 1/2 teaspoon dried thyme
- 1/2 teaspoon sugar
- Fresh parsley, chopped (for garnish)

Instructions:

Cook the linguine according to the package instructions in a large pot of salted boiling water. Drain and set aside.
Season the shrimp with salt and black pepper.
In a large skillet, heat olive oil over medium-high heat. Add minced garlic and red pepper flakes, sautéing for about 1 minute until the garlic becomes fragrant.
Add the seasoned shrimp to the skillet and cook for 2-3 minutes per side or until they are pink and opaque. Remove the shrimp from the skillet and set aside.
In the same skillet, pour in the dry white wine, scraping up any browned bits from the bottom.
Stir in crushed tomatoes, dried oregano, dried basil, dried thyme, and sugar.
Simmer the sauce for about 10-15 minutes, allowing it to thicken.
Return the cooked shrimp to the skillet, tossing them in the spicy tomato sauce.
Serve the Shrimp Fra Diavolo over the cooked linguine, garnished with chopped fresh parsley.

Enjoy your spicy and flavorful Shrimp Fra Diavolo! Adjust the level of red pepper flakes to suit your preferred spice level.

Avocado Pesto Pasta

Ingredients:

For the Avocado Pesto:

- 2 ripe avocados, peeled and pitted
- 1 cup fresh basil leaves
- 1/2 cup grated Parmesan cheese
- 1/3 cup pine nuts
- 2 cloves garlic, minced
- 1/2 cup extra-virgin olive oil
- Salt and black pepper to taste
- Juice of 1 lemon

For the Pasta:

- 8 oz (225g) spaghetti or your favorite pasta
- Cherry tomatoes, halved (optional, for garnish)
- Fresh basil leaves, chopped (for garnish)
- Grated Parmesan cheese (for serving)

Instructions:

Cook the pasta according to the package instructions in a large pot of salted boiling water. Reserve about 1 cup of pasta cooking water before draining.

In a food processor, combine the peeled and pitted avocados, fresh basil leaves, grated Parmesan cheese, pine nuts, minced garlic, and lemon juice. Pulse until the ingredients are well combined.

With the food processor running, slowly pour in the extra-virgin olive oil until the mixture becomes smooth and creamy. Season with salt and black pepper to taste. Adjust the consistency with pasta cooking water if needed.

Toss the cooked pasta with the avocado pesto in a large bowl, ensuring it is well coated.

Garnish the Avocado Pesto Pasta with halved cherry tomatoes, chopped fresh basil leaves, and grated Parmesan cheese.

Serve the pasta immediately, enjoying the creamy and vibrant flavors of the Avocado Pesto.

This dish is not only delicious but also provides a unique twist on traditional pesto. Enjoy your Avocado Pesto Pasta!

Chicken and Broccoli Alfredo

Ingredients:

- 8 oz (225g) fettuccine or your favorite pasta
- 1 pound (450g) boneless, skinless chicken breasts, cut into bite-sized pieces
- Salt and black pepper to taste
- 2 tablespoons olive oil
- 3 cloves garlic, minced
- 2 cups broccoli florets, blanched
- 1 cup (240ml) heavy cream
- 1 cup (100g) grated Parmesan cheese
- 2 tablespoons unsalted butter
- Salt and black pepper to taste
- Fresh parsley, chopped (for garnish)

Instructions:

Cook the fettuccine according to the package instructions in a large pot of salted boiling water. Reserve about 1 cup of pasta cooking water before draining.
Season the chicken pieces with salt and black pepper.
In a large skillet, heat olive oil over medium-high heat. Add the seasoned chicken and cook until browned on all sides and cooked through. Remove the chicken from the skillet and set aside.
In the same skillet, add minced garlic and sauté for about 1-2 minutes until fragrant.
Pour in heavy cream, grated Parmesan cheese, and unsalted butter. Stir well to combine and let the sauce simmer for 3-4 minutes until it thickens.
Add blanched broccoli to the Alfredo sauce and toss to combine.
Return the cooked chicken to the skillet, allowing it to heat through in the sauce.
Toss the cooked fettuccine into the skillet, coating it evenly with the Chicken and Broccoli Alfredo sauce. If needed, add a bit of the reserved pasta cooking water to achieve the desired consistency.
Season with additional salt and black pepper if necessary.
Serve the Chicken and Broccoli Alfredo hot, garnished with chopped fresh parsley.

Enjoy your creamy and comforting Chicken and Broccoli Alfredo!

Crab Linguine

Ingredients:

- 8 oz (225g) linguine or your favorite pasta
- 2 tablespoons olive oil
- 3 cloves garlic, minced
- 1/2 teaspoon red pepper flakes (adjust to taste)
- 1 pound (450g) fresh or canned crab meat, picked over for shells
- 1 cup cherry tomatoes, halved
- 1/4 cup dry white wine
- Zest and juice of 1 lemon
- 1/4 cup fresh parsley, chopped
- Salt and black pepper to taste
- Grated Parmesan cheese (for serving)

Instructions:

Cook the linguine according to the package instructions in a large pot of salted boiling water. Reserve about 1 cup of pasta cooking water before draining.
In a large skillet, heat olive oil over medium heat. Add minced garlic and red pepper flakes, sautéing for about 1-2 minutes until the garlic becomes fragrant.
Add the crab meat to the skillet and gently toss to heat through.
Pour in dry white wine, allowing it to simmer for 1-2 minutes to cook off the alcohol.
Add halved cherry tomatoes, lemon zest, and lemon juice to the skillet. Toss to combine.
Toss the cooked linguine into the skillet, coating it evenly with the crab and tomato mixture. If needed, add a bit of the reserved pasta cooking water to achieve the desired consistency.
Season with salt and black pepper to taste. Stir in chopped fresh parsley.
Serve the Crab Linguine hot, garnished with grated Parmesan cheese.

Enjoy your delicious and elegant Crab Linguine! The delicate crab flavor pairs wonderfully with the brightness of lemon and the sweetness of tomatoes.

Spaghetti Aglio, Olio e Peperoncino

Ingredients:

- 8 oz (225g) spaghetti
- 1/3 cup extra-virgin olive oil
- 4 cloves garlic, thinly sliced
- 1/2 teaspoon red pepper flakes (adjust to taste)
- Salt to taste
- Chopped fresh parsley (for garnish)
- Grated Parmesan cheese (optional, for serving)

Instructions:

Cook the spaghetti according to the package instructions in a large pot of salted boiling water. Reserve about 1 cup of pasta cooking water before draining.

In a large skillet, heat extra-virgin olive oil over medium heat. Add thinly sliced garlic and red pepper flakes, sautéing for about 1-2 minutes until the garlic becomes golden but not browned.

Add cooked and drained spaghetti to the skillet, tossing it to coat evenly with the garlic-infused olive oil.

If the pasta seems dry, add a bit of the reserved pasta cooking water to achieve the desired consistency.

Season with salt to taste and continue to toss the spaghetti until it is well coated with the garlic and red pepper flakes.

Garnish with chopped fresh parsley.

Optionally, serve Spaghetti Aglio, Olio e Peperoncino with grated Parmesan cheese on the side.

Enjoy your quick and delicious Spaghetti Aglio, Olio e Peperoncino! This dish celebrates the simplicity of a few quality ingredients.

Pumpkin Sage Pasta

Ingredients:

- 8 oz (225g) pasta (penne, fettuccine, or your choice)
- 1 cup canned pumpkin puree
- 1/2 cup heavy cream
- 1/2 cup grated Parmesan cheese
- 2 tablespoons unsalted butter
- 1 tablespoon olive oil
- 2 cloves garlic, minced
- 8-10 fresh sage leaves, chopped
- Salt and black pepper to taste
- Pinch of nutmeg (optional)
- Toasted pine nuts (for garnish, optional)

Instructions:

Cook the pasta according to the package instructions in a large pot of salted boiling water. Reserve about 1 cup of pasta cooking water before draining.
In a skillet, melt butter and olive oil over medium heat. Add minced garlic and chopped fresh sage leaves, sautéing for about 1-2 minutes until fragrant.
Stir in the canned pumpkin puree, heavy cream, and grated Parmesan cheese. Mix well until the cheese is melted and the sauce becomes smooth.
If the sauce is too thick, add a bit of the reserved pasta cooking water to achieve the desired consistency.
Season the pumpkin sauce with salt, black pepper, and a pinch of nutmeg (if using). Adjust the seasoning to your taste.
Toss the cooked pasta into the skillet, ensuring it is well coated with the pumpkin and sage sauce.
Serve the Pumpkin Sage Pasta hot, garnished with additional grated Parmesan cheese and toasted pine nuts if desired.

Enjoy your comforting and flavorful Pumpkin Sage Pasta! It's a perfect dish for the fall season.

Mediterranean Orzo Salad

Ingredients:

For the Salad:

- 1 cup orzo pasta
- 1 cup cherry tomatoes, halved
- 1 cucumber, diced
- 1/2 red onion, finely chopped
- 1/2 cup Kalamata olives, sliced
- 1/2 cup crumbled feta cheese
- 1/4 cup fresh parsley, chopped
- 1/4 cup fresh basil, chopped

For the Dressing:

- 1/4 cup extra-virgin olive oil
- 2 tablespoons red wine vinegar
- 1 teaspoon Dijon mustard
- 1 clove garlic, minced
- Salt and black pepper to taste

Instructions:

Cook the orzo pasta according to the package instructions in a large pot of salted boiling water. Drain and rinse under cold water to cool.

In a large bowl, combine the cooked and cooled orzo with halved cherry tomatoes, diced cucumber, finely chopped red onion, sliced Kalamata olives, crumbled feta cheese, chopped fresh parsley, and chopped fresh basil.

In a small bowl, whisk together the dressing ingredients: extra-virgin olive oil, red wine vinegar, Dijon mustard, minced garlic, salt, and black pepper.

Pour the dressing over the orzo salad ingredients and toss everything together until well combined.

Adjust the seasoning to taste, and chill the Mediterranean Orzo Salad in the refrigerator for at least 30 minutes before serving.

Before serving, give the salad a final toss and garnish with additional fresh herbs.

Enjoy your light and flavorful Mediterranean Orzo Salad! It's a perfect side dish for picnics, barbecues, or a light lunch.

Buffalo Chicken Mac and Cheese

Ingredients:

- 8 oz (225g) elbow macaroni or your favorite pasta
- 2 cups shredded cooked chicken (rotisserie chicken works well)
- 1/2 cup buffalo sauce
- 1/4 cup unsalted butter
- 1/4 cup all-purpose flour
- 2 cups whole milk
- 2 cups shredded sharp cheddar cheese
- 1 cup shredded mozzarella cheese
- 1/2 cup blue cheese crumbles
- Salt and black pepper to taste
- Green onions, chopped (for garnish, optional)
- Celery sticks (for serving, optional)

Instructions:

Cook the macaroni according to the package instructions in a large pot of salted boiling water. Drain and set aside.

In a large skillet or saucepan, melt the butter over medium heat. Stir in the flour to create a roux and cook for 1-2 minutes until it's lightly golden.

Gradually whisk in the milk, stirring continuously to avoid lumps. Cook until the mixture thickens, about 5 minutes.

Reduce the heat to low, and add the shredded cheddar cheese, mozzarella cheese, and blue cheese crumbles. Stir until the cheeses are melted and the sauce is smooth.

Add the shredded chicken and buffalo sauce to the cheese sauce, stirring until the chicken is well coated.

Season the sauce with salt and black pepper to taste.

Toss the cooked macaroni into the buffalo chicken and cheese sauce, coating it evenly.

Serve the Buffalo Chicken Mac and Cheese hot, garnished with chopped green onions if desired.

Optionally, serve with celery sticks on the side for a touch of freshness.

Enjoy your indulgent and spicy Buffalo Chicken Mac and Cheese!

Chicken and Asparagus Lemon Pasta

Ingredients:

- 8 oz (225g) linguine or your favorite pasta
- 1 pound (450g) boneless, skinless chicken breasts, thinly sliced
- Salt and black pepper to taste
- 2 tablespoons olive oil
- 1 bunch asparagus, trimmed and cut into bite-sized pieces
- 3 cloves garlic, minced
- Zest and juice of 1 lemon
- 1 cup (240ml) chicken broth
- 1/2 cup (120ml) heavy cream
- 1/2 cup grated Parmesan cheese
- Fresh parsley, chopped (for garnish)

Instructions:

Cook the linguine according to the package instructions in a large pot of salted boiling water. Reserve about 1 cup of pasta cooking water before draining.
Season the thinly sliced chicken with salt and black pepper.
In a large skillet, heat olive oil over medium-high heat. Add the seasoned chicken and cook until browned on all sides and cooked through. Remove the chicken from the skillet and set aside.
In the same skillet, add asparagus pieces and sauté for about 3-4 minutes until they are bright green and slightly tender.
Add minced garlic to the skillet and sauté for about 1 minute until it becomes fragrant.
Pour in chicken broth, heavy cream, lemon zest, and lemon juice. Bring the mixture to a simmer.
Stir in grated Parmesan cheese until the sauce is smooth.
Return the cooked chicken to the skillet, tossing it in the lemony asparagus sauce.
Toss the cooked linguine into the skillet, coating it evenly with the Chicken and Asparagus Lemon Pasta. If needed, add a bit of the reserved pasta cooking water to achieve the desired consistency.
Season with additional salt and black pepper if necessary.
Serve the Chicken and Asparagus Lemon Pasta hot, garnished with chopped fresh parsley.

Enjoy your light and flavorful Chicken and Asparagus Lemon Pasta!

Rigatoni with Sausage and Kale

Ingredients:

- 8 oz (225g) rigatoni or your favorite pasta
- 1 pound (450g) Italian sausage, casings removed
- 2 tablespoons olive oil
- 1 onion, finely chopped
- 3 cloves garlic, minced
- 1 bunch kale, stems removed and leaves chopped
- 1 can (14 oz) diced tomatoes
- 1 teaspoon dried oregano
- 1 teaspoon dried basil
- Salt and black pepper to taste
- Red pepper flakes (optional, for heat)
- Grated Parmesan cheese (for serving)

Instructions:

Cook the rigatoni according to the package instructions in a large pot of salted boiling water. Reserve about 1 cup of pasta cooking water before draining.
In a large skillet, heat olive oil over medium heat. Add the Italian sausage, breaking it up with a spoon, and cook until browned and cooked through. Remove excess fat if necessary.
Add chopped onion to the skillet and sauté until it becomes translucent.
Stir in minced garlic and chopped kale. Cook for about 3-4 minutes until the kale wilts.
Pour in diced tomatoes (with their juice), dried oregano, and dried basil. Season with salt, black pepper, and red pepper flakes (if using). Simmer the sauce for about 10 minutes.
Toss the cooked rigatoni into the skillet, coating it evenly with the sausage and kale sauce. If needed, add a bit of the reserved pasta cooking water to achieve the desired consistency.
Adjust the seasoning if necessary.
Serve the Rigatoni with Sausage and Kale hot, garnished with grated Parmesan cheese.

Enjoy your hearty and comforting Rigatoni with Sausage and Kale!

Shrimp and Bacon Carbonara

Ingredients:

- 8 oz (225g) spaghetti or your favorite pasta
- 6 slices bacon, chopped
- 1 pound (450g) large shrimp, peeled and deveined
- 3 cloves garlic, minced
- 3 large eggs
- 1 cup (100g) grated Parmesan cheese
- Salt and black pepper to taste
- Fresh parsley, chopped (for garnish)

Instructions:

Cook the spaghetti according to the package instructions in a large pot of salted boiling water. Reserve about 1 cup of pasta cooking water before draining.
In a large skillet over medium heat, cook the chopped bacon until it becomes crispy. Remove the bacon from the skillet and set it aside.
In the same skillet, add the peeled and deveined shrimp. Cook until the shrimp turn pink and opaque, about 2-3 minutes per side. Remove the shrimp from the skillet and set them aside.
In a bowl, whisk together the eggs, grated Parmesan cheese, minced garlic, salt, and black pepper.
Toss the cooked and drained spaghetti into the skillet with the bacon drippings, ensuring the pasta is well coated.
Pour the egg and Parmesan mixture over the spaghetti, tossing quickly to create a creamy sauce. If needed, add a bit of the reserved pasta cooking water to achieve the desired consistency.
Add the cooked shrimp and crispy bacon to the skillet, tossing them with the pasta until well combined.
Serve the Shrimp and Bacon Carbonara hot, garnished with chopped fresh parsley.

Enjoy your delicious and indulgent Shrimp and Bacon Carbonara!

Lemon Butter Shrimp Pasta

Ingredients:

- 8 oz (225g) linguine or your favorite pasta
- 1 pound (450g) large shrimp, peeled and deveined
- Salt and black pepper to taste
- 2 tablespoons olive oil
- 4 tablespoons unsalted butter
- 3 cloves garlic, minced
- Zest and juice of 2 lemons
- 1/2 cup chicken broth
- 1/4 cup heavy cream
- Red pepper flakes (optional, for heat)
- Fresh parsley, chopped (for garnish)
- Grated Parmesan cheese (optional, for serving)

Instructions:

Cook the linguine according to the package instructions in a large pot of salted boiling water. Reserve about 1 cup of pasta cooking water before draining.
Season the peeled and deveined shrimp with salt and black pepper.
In a large skillet, heat olive oil over medium-high heat. Add the seasoned shrimp and cook for 2-3 minutes per side or until they are pink and opaque. Remove the shrimp from the skillet and set aside.
In the same skillet, melt unsalted butter. Add minced garlic and sauté for about 1-2 minutes until fragrant.
Pour in chicken broth, lemon zest, and lemon juice. Bring the mixture to a simmer.
Stir in heavy cream and red pepper flakes (if using). Simmer for an additional 2-3 minutes until the sauce thickens slightly.
Toss the cooked linguine into the skillet, coating it evenly with the lemon butter sauce. If needed, add a bit of the reserved pasta cooking water to achieve the desired consistency.
Return the cooked shrimp to the skillet, tossing them with the pasta in the lemon butter sauce.
Season with additional salt and black pepper if necessary.
Serve the Lemon Butter Shrimp Pasta hot, garnished with chopped fresh parsley.

Enjoy your bright and flavorful Lemon Butter Shrimp Pasta! Optionally, sprinkle with grated Parmesan cheese before serving for an extra touch of richness.

Mediterranean Vegetable Pasta

Ingredients:

- 8 oz (225g) penne or your favorite pasta
- 3 tablespoons olive oil
- 3 cloves garlic, minced
- 1 eggplant, diced
- 1 zucchini, diced
- 1 red bell pepper, diced
- 1 yellow bell pepper, diced
- 1 pint (about 2 cups) cherry tomatoes, halved
- 1 teaspoon dried oregano
- 1 teaspoon dried basil
- Salt and black pepper to taste
- 1/2 cup Kalamata olives, sliced
- 1/4 cup fresh parsley, chopped
- 1/4 cup feta cheese, crumbled (optional)
- Lemon wedges (for serving)

Instructions:

Cook the penne according to the package instructions in a large pot of salted boiling water. Reserve about 1 cup of pasta cooking water before draining.

In a large skillet, heat olive oil over medium heat. Add minced garlic and sauté for about 1 minute until fragrant.

Add diced eggplant, zucchini, red bell pepper, and yellow bell pepper to the skillet. Sauté for 8-10 minutes or until the vegetables are tender.

Stir in cherry tomatoes, dried oregano, dried basil, salt, and black pepper. Cook for an additional 5 minutes, allowing the tomatoes to soften.

Toss the cooked and drained penne into the skillet, coating it evenly with the Mediterranean vegetable mixture. If needed, add a bit of the reserved pasta cooking water to achieve the desired consistency.

Add sliced Kalamata olives and chopped fresh parsley to the pasta, tossing to combine.

Optionally, sprinkle crumbled feta cheese over the Mediterranean Vegetable Pasta before serving.

Serve the pasta hot, accompanied by lemon wedges for a touch of brightness.

Enjoy your colorful and delicious Mediterranean Vegetable Pasta, a celebration of fresh and wholesome ingredients!

Gnocchi with Brown Butter and Sage

Ingredients:

- 1 pound (about 450g) store-bought gnocchi or homemade gnocchi
- 1/2 cup (1 stick) unsalted butter
- Fresh sage leaves
- Salt and black pepper to taste
- Grated Parmesan cheese (for serving, optional)

Instructions:

Cook the gnocchi according to the package instructions or your homemade gnocchi recipe. Typically, gnocchi are done when they float to the surface of the boiling water. Drain and set aside.
In a large skillet, melt the butter over medium heat. Once melted, continue cooking until the butter turns a golden brown color, and you can smell a nutty aroma. Be careful not to burn it.
Add fresh sage leaves to the brown butter and fry them until they become crispy, about 1-2 minutes. Use a slotted spoon to remove the sage leaves and set them aside.
Add the cooked gnocchi to the skillet with the brown butter, tossing them gently to coat evenly. Allow the gnocchi to cook for a couple of minutes, developing a slight crispness on the edges.
Season the gnocchi with salt and black pepper to taste.
Serve the Gnocchi with Brown Butter and Sage hot, garnished with the crispy sage leaves. Optionally, sprinkle with grated Parmesan cheese before serving.

Enjoy your delightful and indulgent Gnocchi with Brown Butter and Sage!

Chicken Marsala Pasta

Ingredients:

- 8 oz (225g) fettuccine or your favorite pasta
- 2 boneless, skinless chicken breasts, thinly sliced
- Salt and black pepper to taste
- 1/2 cup all-purpose flour, for dredging
- 4 tablespoons olive oil
- 8 oz (225g) cremini or button mushrooms, sliced
- 3 cloves garlic, minced
- 1 cup Marsala wine
- 1 cup chicken broth
- 2 tablespoons unsalted butter
- Fresh parsley, chopped (for garnish)
- Grated Parmesan cheese (for serving)

Instructions:

Cook the fettuccine according to the package instructions in a large pot of salted boiling water. Reserve about 1 cup of pasta cooking water before draining.

Season the thinly sliced chicken with salt and black pepper, then dredge in flour, shaking off excess.

In a large skillet, heat olive oil over medium-high heat. Add the chicken slices and cook until browned on both sides and cooked through. Remove the chicken from the skillet and set aside.

In the same skillet, add sliced mushrooms and sauté until they release their moisture and become golden brown.

Add minced garlic to the skillet and sauté for about 1-2 minutes until fragrant.

Pour in Marsala wine and chicken broth, scraping up any browned bits from the bottom of the skillet. Bring the mixture to a simmer.

Return the cooked chicken to the skillet, allowing it to heat through in the Marsala sauce.

Toss the cooked fettuccine into the skillet, coating it evenly with the Chicken Marsala sauce. If needed, add a bit of the reserved pasta cooking water to achieve the desired consistency.

Stir in unsalted butter until the sauce is creamy and well combined.

Season with additional salt and black pepper if necessary.

Serve the Chicken Marsala Pasta hot, garnished with chopped fresh parsley and grated Parmesan cheese.

Enjoy your flavorful and satisfying Chicken Marsala Pasta!

Shrimp and Avocado Pasta Salad

Ingredients:

For the Salad:

- 8 oz (225g) fusilli or your favorite pasta
- 1 pound (450g) large shrimp, peeled and deveined
- 1 tablespoon olive oil
- Salt and black pepper to taste
- 2 avocados, diced
- 1 cup cherry tomatoes, halved
- 1/4 cup red onion, finely chopped
- 1/4 cup fresh cilantro, chopped

For the Dressing:

- 3 tablespoons extra-virgin olive oil
- 2 tablespoons fresh lime juice
- 1 teaspoon honey
- 1 clove garlic, minced
- Salt and black pepper to taste

Instructions:

Cook the fusilli according to the package instructions in a large pot of salted boiling water. Reserve about 1 cup of pasta cooking water before draining.
In a large skillet, heat olive oil over medium-high heat. Season the peeled and deveined shrimp with salt and black pepper. Cook the shrimp for 2-3 minutes per side or until they are pink and opaque. Remove the shrimp from the skillet and set aside.
In a large bowl, combine the cooked and drained fusilli with diced avocado, halved cherry tomatoes, chopped red onion, and chopped cilantro.
In a small bowl, whisk together the dressing ingredients: extra-virgin olive oil, fresh lime juice, honey, minced garlic, salt, and black pepper.
Pour the dressing over the pasta and vegetable mixture, tossing gently to coat.
Add the cooked shrimp to the salad, tossing to combine.
If needed, add a bit of the reserved pasta cooking water to achieve the desired consistency.

Serve the Shrimp and Avocado Pasta Salad chilled.

Enjoy your light and flavorful Shrimp and Avocado Pasta Salad! It's perfect for a refreshing lunch or dinner.

Creamy Tomato and Basil Tortellini

Ingredients:

- 1 pound (450g) cheese tortellini
- 2 tablespoons olive oil
- 1 onion, finely chopped
- 3 cloves garlic, minced
- 1 can (28 oz) crushed tomatoes
- 1 teaspoon dried basil
- 1/2 teaspoon dried oregano
- 1/2 teaspoon red pepper flakes (optional, for heat)
- Salt and black pepper to taste
- 1 cup heavy cream
- 1/2 cup grated Parmesan cheese
- Fresh basil, chopped (for garnish)

Instructions:

Cook the cheese tortellini according to the package instructions in a large pot of salted boiling water. Reserve about 1 cup of pasta cooking water before draining. In a large skillet, heat olive oil over medium heat. Add chopped onion and sauté until it becomes translucent.

Add minced garlic to the skillet and sauté for about 1-2 minutes until fragrant.

Pour in crushed tomatoes, dried basil, dried oregano, red pepper flakes (if using), salt, and black pepper. Simmer the sauce for about 10-15 minutes, allowing it to thicken.

Stir in heavy cream and grated Parmesan cheese. Cook for an additional 2-3 minutes until the sauce is creamy and well combined.

Toss the cooked and drained tortellini into the skillet, coating it evenly with the Creamy Tomato and Basil sauce. If needed, add a bit of the reserved pasta cooking water to achieve the desired consistency.

Season with additional salt and black pepper if necessary.

Serve the Creamy Tomato and Basil Tortellini hot, garnished with chopped fresh basil.

Enjoy your delicious and indulgent Creamy Tomato and Basil Tortellini!

Baked Rigatoni with Meatballs

Ingredients:

For the Meatballs:

- 1 pound (450g) ground beef
- 1/2 cup breadcrumbs
- 1/4 cup grated Parmesan cheese
- 1/4 cup chopped fresh parsley
- 1 egg
- 2 cloves garlic, minced
- Salt and black pepper to taste

For the Tomato Sauce:

- 2 tablespoons olive oil
- 1 onion, finely chopped
- 3 cloves garlic, minced
- 1 can (28 oz) crushed tomatoes
- 1 teaspoon dried oregano
- 1 teaspoon dried basil
- Salt and black pepper to taste
- Pinch of sugar (optional, to balance acidity)

For the Baked Rigatoni:

- 1 pound (450g) rigatoni
- 2 cups shredded mozzarella cheese
- Fresh basil, chopped (for garnish)

Instructions:

Preheat the oven to 375°F (190°C).
In a large bowl, combine all the meatball ingredients: ground beef, breadcrumbs, grated Parmesan cheese, chopped fresh parsley, egg, minced garlic, salt, and black pepper. Mix until well combined.
Shape the mixture into meatballs, about 1 to 1.5 inches in diameter.
In a large skillet, heat olive oil over medium heat. Add chopped onion and sauté until it becomes translucent.

Add minced garlic to the skillet and sauté for about 1-2 minutes until fragrant. Pour in crushed tomatoes, dried oregano, dried basil, salt, black pepper, and a pinch of sugar (if using). Simmer the sauce for about 15-20 minutes, allowing it to thicken.

While the sauce is simmering, cook the rigatoni according to the package instructions in a large pot of salted boiling water. Drain and set aside.

In the tomato sauce, add the meatballs, allowing them to simmer for an additional 10-15 minutes until they are cooked through.

In a large baking dish, combine the cooked rigatoni with the meatball and tomato sauce mixture. Toss until the pasta is well coated.

Sprinkle shredded mozzarella cheese over the top of the rigatoni.

Bake in the preheated oven for 20-25 minutes or until the cheese is melted and bubbly.

Garnish with chopped fresh basil before serving.

Enjoy your delicious and comforting Baked Rigatoni with Meatballs!

Garlic Parmesan Pasta

Ingredients:

- 8 oz (225g) linguine or your favorite pasta
- 3 tablespoons unsalted butter
- 4 cloves garlic, minced
- 1 cup heavy cream
- 1 cup grated Parmesan cheese
- Salt and black pepper to taste
- Chopped fresh parsley (for garnish)
- Red pepper flakes (optional, for heat)

Instructions:

Cook the linguine according to the package instructions in a large pot of salted boiling water. Reserve about 1 cup of pasta cooking water before draining.
In a large skillet, melt the unsalted butter over medium heat. Add minced garlic and sauté for about 1-2 minutes until fragrant.
Pour in heavy cream, stirring continuously. Bring the mixture to a simmer.
Gradually whisk in grated Parmesan cheese, ensuring it melts into the sauce and becomes smooth.
If the sauce is too thick, add a bit of the reserved pasta cooking water to achieve the desired consistency.
Season the sauce with salt and black pepper to taste. Add red pepper flakes if you like a bit of heat.
Toss the cooked linguine into the skillet, coating it evenly with the creamy Garlic Parmesan sauce.
Serve the Garlic Parmesan Pasta hot, garnished with chopped fresh parsley.

Enjoy your quick and delightful Garlic Parmesan Pasta! It's a perfect option for a simple and satisfying meal.

Sweet Potato Gnocchi

Ingredients:

For the Sweet Potato Gnocchi:

- 2 medium-sized sweet potatoes (about 1 pound or 450g)
- 1 cup ricotta cheese
- 1/2 cup grated Parmesan cheese
- 1 large egg
- 1 teaspoon salt
- 2 to 2 1/2 cups all-purpose flour, plus more for dusting

For Cooking and Serving:

- Salt for boiling water
- Olive oil or butter for sautéing
- Sage leaves for garnish (optional)
- Grated Parmesan cheese for serving

Instructions:

Preheat the oven to 400°F (200°C). Pierce the sweet potatoes with a fork and bake them on a baking sheet for about 45-60 minutes or until they are fork-tender.

Allow the sweet potatoes to cool slightly, then peel off the skin and mash them in a large bowl. Let the mashed sweet potatoes cool completely.

Once the sweet potatoes are cooled, add ricotta cheese, grated Parmesan cheese, egg, and salt. Mix well until the ingredients are combined.

Gradually add the flour, one cup at a time, mixing until a soft dough forms. The amount of flour may vary, so add enough to achieve a workable and not too sticky consistency.

Turn the dough out onto a floured surface. Divide it into four portions.

Roll each portion into a long rope, about 1/2 inch in diameter. Cut each rope into bite-sized pieces.

If desired, you can create ridges on each gnocchi by rolling them over the back of a fork or using a gnocchi board.

Bring a large pot of salted water to a boil. Drop the gnocchi into the boiling water in batches. Cook until they float to the surface, which usually takes about 2-3 minutes. Remove them with a slotted spoon and set aside.

In a separate pan, heat olive oil or butter over medium heat. Sauté the cooked gnocchi until they are lightly browned.
Serve the Sweet Potato Gnocchi hot, garnished with sage leaves and grated Parmesan cheese.

Enjoy your homemade Sweet Potato Gnocchi, a flavorful and comforting dish!

Italian Sausage and Peppers Cavatappi

Ingredients:

- 12 oz (340g) cavatappi or your favorite pasta
- 1 pound (450g) Italian sausage, casings removed
- 2 tablespoons olive oil
- 1 onion, thinly sliced
- 3 bell peppers (red, yellow, and green), thinly sliced
- 3 cloves garlic, minced
- 1 can (28 oz) crushed tomatoes
- 1 teaspoon dried oregano
- 1 teaspoon dried basil
- 1/2 teaspoon red pepper flakes (optional, for heat)
- Salt and black pepper to taste
- Fresh basil, chopped (for garnish)
- Grated Parmesan cheese (for serving)

Instructions:

Cook the cavatappi according to the package instructions in a large pot of salted boiling water. Reserve about 1 cup of pasta cooking water before draining.

In a large skillet, heat olive oil over medium-high heat. Add the Italian sausage, breaking it up with a spoon, and cook until browned and cooked through. Remove excess fat if necessary.

Add thinly sliced onion and bell peppers to the skillet. Sauté until the vegetables are softened.

Stir in minced garlic and cook for about 1-2 minutes until fragrant.

Pour in crushed tomatoes, dried oregano, dried basil, red pepper flakes (if using), salt, and black pepper. Simmer the sauce for about 10-15 minutes, allowing it to thicken.

Toss the cooked and drained cavatappi into the skillet, coating it evenly with the Italian Sausage and Peppers sauce. If needed, add a bit of the reserved pasta cooking water to achieve the desired consistency.

Adjust the seasoning if necessary.

Serve the Italian Sausage and Peppers Cavatappi hot, garnished with chopped fresh basil and grated Parmesan cheese.

Enjoy your delicious and hearty Italian Sausage and Peppers Cavatappi!

Shrimp and Zucchini Noodles

Ingredients:

- 1 pound (450g) large shrimp, peeled and deveined
- 3 medium zucchini, spiralized into noodles
- 2 tablespoons olive oil
- 4 cloves garlic, minced
- 1 teaspoon red pepper flakes (optional, for heat)
- Salt and black pepper to taste
- Juice of 1 lemon
- 2 tablespoons fresh parsley, chopped
- Grated Parmesan cheese (for serving)

Instructions:

In a large skillet, heat olive oil over medium-high heat. Add minced garlic and red pepper flakes (if using) and sauté for about 1-2 minutes until fragrant.
Add the peeled and deveined shrimp to the skillet. Cook for 2-3 minutes per side or until they are pink and opaque. Remove the shrimp from the skillet and set aside.
In the same skillet, add the spiralized zucchini noodles. Sauté for 2-3 minutes until they are just tender but still have a bit of crunch.
Season the zucchini noodles with salt and black pepper to taste.
Return the cooked shrimp to the skillet, tossing them with the zucchini noodles.
Drizzle the lemon juice over the shrimp and zucchini noodles, tossing to combine.
Stir in chopped fresh parsley.
Serve the Shrimp and Zucchini Noodles hot, optionally topped with grated Parmesan cheese.

Enjoy your light and flavorful Shrimp and Zucchini Noodles, a perfect dish for a healthy and satisfying meal!

Roasted Red Pepper and Goat Cheese Pasta

Ingredients:

- 8 oz (225g) penne or your favorite pasta
- 2 large red bell peppers
- 2 tablespoons olive oil
- 1 onion, finely chopped
- 3 cloves garlic, minced
- 4 oz (113g) goat cheese, crumbled
- 1/2 cup grated Parmesan cheese
- Salt and black pepper to taste
- Crushed red pepper flakes (optional, for heat)
- Fresh basil, chopped (for garnish)

Instructions:

Preheat the oven to 400°F (200°C).

Cut the red bell peppers into quarters, removing the seeds and membranes.

Place them on a baking sheet, skin side up. Drizzle with olive oil.

Roast the red peppers in the preheated oven for about 20-25 minutes or until the skins are charred and blistered.

Remove the roasted red peppers from the oven and let them cool slightly. Peel off the charred skins.

In a blender or food processor, combine the roasted red peppers and blend until smooth. Set aside.

Cook the penne according to the package instructions in a large pot of salted boiling water. Reserve about 1 cup of pasta cooking water before draining.

In a large skillet, heat olive oil over medium heat. Add finely chopped onion and sauté until it becomes translucent.

Add minced garlic to the skillet and sauté for about 1-2 minutes until fragrant.

Pour in the blended roasted red pepper sauce, stirring to combine with the onion and garlic.

Add crumbled goat cheese and grated Parmesan cheese to the skillet. Stir until the cheeses melt into the sauce.

Season the sauce with salt, black pepper, and crushed red pepper flakes (if using).

Toss the cooked and drained penne into the skillet, coating it evenly with the Roasted Red Pepper and Goat Cheese sauce. If needed, add a bit of the reserved pasta cooking water to achieve the desired consistency.
Serve the pasta hot, garnished with chopped fresh basil.

Enjoy your delicious and creamy Roasted Red Pepper and Goat Cheese Pasta!

Chicken Alfredo Stuffed Shells

Ingredients:

For the Stuffed Shells:

- 24 jumbo pasta shells
- 2 cups cooked chicken, shredded or diced
- 2 cups ricotta cheese
- 1 cup shredded mozzarella cheese
- 1/2 cup grated Parmesan cheese
- 2 cloves garlic, minced
- 1/4 cup fresh parsley, chopped
- Salt and black pepper to taste

For the Alfredo Sauce:

- 1/2 cup unsalted butter
- 1 cup heavy cream
- 2 cups grated Parmesan cheese
- Salt and black pepper to taste
- 1/2 teaspoon garlic powder (optional)

Instructions:

Preheat the oven to 375°F (190°C).
Cook the jumbo pasta shells according to the package instructions in a large pot of salted boiling water. Drain and set aside.
In a large bowl, combine the cooked and shredded chicken, ricotta cheese, shredded mozzarella cheese, grated Parmesan cheese, minced garlic, chopped fresh parsley, salt, and black pepper. Mix well.
In a saucepan, melt unsalted butter over medium heat. Add heavy cream and bring it to a simmer.
Gradually whisk in grated Parmesan cheese, stirring until the sauce is smooth. Season with salt, black pepper, and garlic powder (if using). Simmer for a few minutes until the sauce thickens.
Spread a thin layer of Alfredo sauce on the bottom of a baking dish.
Stuff each jumbo pasta shell with the chicken and cheese mixture, arranging them in the baking dish.

Pour the remaining Alfredo sauce over the stuffed shells, ensuring they are well covered.
Sprinkle extra grated Parmesan cheese on top if desired.
Bake in the preheated oven for 25-30 minutes or until the shells are heated through and the top is golden brown.
Remove from the oven and let it cool for a few minutes before serving.
Garnish with additional chopped fresh parsley if desired.

Enjoy your creamy and satisfying Chicken Alfredo Stuffed Shells!

Shrimp and Scallop Linguine

Ingredients:

- 8 oz (225g) linguine or your favorite pasta
- 1/2 pound (225g) large shrimp, peeled and deveined
- 1/2 pound (225g) sea scallops, side muscle removed
- 2 tablespoons olive oil
- 4 cloves garlic, minced
- 1/2 cup dry white wine
- 1 cup cherry tomatoes, halved
- Zest and juice of 1 lemon
- 1/4 cup fresh parsley, chopped
- Salt and black pepper to taste
- Red pepper flakes (optional, for heat)
- Grated Parmesan cheese (for serving)

Instructions:

Cook the linguine according to the package instructions in a large pot of salted boiling water. Reserve about 1 cup of pasta cooking water before draining.
In a large skillet, heat olive oil over medium-high heat. Add minced garlic and sauté for about 1-2 minutes until fragrant.
Add the peeled and deveined shrimp and sea scallops to the skillet. Cook for 2-3 minutes per side or until they are just cooked through.
Pour in dry white wine, scraping up any browned bits from the bottom of the skillet. Allow the wine to simmer and reduce by half.
Add halved cherry tomatoes to the skillet, cooking for an additional 2-3 minutes until they are just softened.
Toss the cooked and drained linguine into the skillet, coating it evenly with the seafood and tomato mixture. If needed, add a bit of the reserved pasta cooking water to achieve the desired consistency.
Zest and juice the lemon over the pasta, and add chopped fresh parsley. Season with salt, black pepper, and red pepper flakes (if using).
Toss everything together until well combined.
Serve the Shrimp and Scallop Linguine hot, optionally sprinkled with grated Parmesan cheese.

Enjoy your elegant and flavorful Shrimp and Scallop Linguine!

Creamy Cajun Chicken and Sausage Pasta

Ingredients:

- 8 oz (225g) penne or your favorite pasta
- 1 pound (450g) boneless, skinless chicken breasts, sliced
- 1/2 pound (225g) smoked sausage, sliced
- 2 tablespoons Cajun seasoning
- 2 tablespoons olive oil
- 1 onion, finely chopped
- 1 bell pepper, thinly sliced
- 3 cloves garlic, minced
- 1 cup cherry tomatoes, halved
- 1 cup heavy cream
- 1/2 cup chicken broth
- Salt and black pepper to taste
- Fresh parsley, chopped (for garnish)

Instructions:

Cook the penne according to the package instructions in a large pot of salted boiling water. Reserve about 1 cup of pasta cooking water before draining.
In a bowl, toss the sliced chicken with Cajun seasoning, ensuring it is well coated.
In a large skillet, heat olive oil over medium-high heat. Add the Cajun-seasoned chicken and cook until browned on all sides and cooked through. Remove the chicken from the skillet and set aside.
In the same skillet, add sliced smoked sausage and cook until it develops a nice brown color. Remove the sausage from the skillet and set aside with the cooked chicken.
In the skillet, add finely chopped onion and thinly sliced bell pepper. Sauté until the vegetables are softened.
Add minced garlic to the skillet and sauté for about 1-2 minutes until fragrant.
Pour in heavy cream and chicken broth, stirring to combine. Bring the mixture to a simmer.
Return the cooked chicken and sausage to the skillet, along with halved cherry tomatoes. Allow it to simmer for 5-7 minutes, letting the flavors meld.
Toss the cooked and drained penne into the skillet, coating it evenly with the Creamy Cajun Chicken and Sausage sauce. If needed, add a bit of the reserved pasta cooking water to achieve the desired consistency.

Season with salt and black pepper to taste.
Serve the Creamy Cajun Chicken and Sausage Pasta hot, garnished with chopped fresh parsley.

Enjoy your rich and flavorful Creamy Cajun Chicken and Sausage Pasta!

Pasta with Eggplant and Tomato Sauce

Ingredients:

- 8 oz (225g) penne or your favorite pasta
- 1 medium-sized eggplant, diced
- Salt
- 3 tablespoons olive oil
- 1 onion, finely chopped
- 2 cloves garlic, minced
- 1 can (28 oz) crushed tomatoes
- 1 teaspoon dried oregano
- 1 teaspoon dried basil
- 1/2 teaspoon red pepper flakes (optional, for heat)
- Black pepper to taste
- Fresh basil, chopped (for garnish)
- Grated Parmesan cheese (for serving)

Instructions:

Cook the penne according to the package instructions in a large pot of salted boiling water. Reserve about 1 cup of pasta cooking water before draining.

Place the diced eggplant in a colander, sprinkle with salt, and let it sit for about 20 minutes. This helps draw out excess moisture and bitterness from the eggplant. After 20 minutes, rinse the eggplant thoroughly and pat it dry with paper towels.

In a large skillet, heat olive oil over medium-high heat. Add chopped onion and sauté until it becomes translucent.

Add minced garlic to the skillet and sauté for about 1-2 minutes until fragrant.

Add the diced and dried eggplant to the skillet. Cook, stirring occasionally, until the eggplant is golden brown and softened.

Pour in crushed tomatoes, dried oregano, dried basil, red pepper flakes (if using), salt, and black pepper. Simmer the sauce for about 15-20 minutes, allowing it to thicken.

Toss the cooked and drained penne into the skillet, coating it evenly with the Eggplant and Tomato sauce. If needed, add a bit of the reserved pasta cooking water to achieve the desired consistency.

Serve the Pasta with Eggplant and Tomato Sauce hot, garnished with chopped fresh basil and grated Parmesan cheese.

Enjoy your flavorful and satisfying Pasta with Eggplant and Tomato Sauce!

Smoked Salmon and Dill Pasta

Ingredients:

- 8 oz (225g) fettuccine or your favorite pasta
- 4 oz (113g) smoked salmon, sliced into strips
- 2 tablespoons olive oil
- 1 shallot, finely chopped
- 2 cloves garlic, minced
- 1/2 cup dry white wine
- 1 cup heavy cream
- Zest and juice of 1 lemon
- 2 tablespoons fresh dill, chopped
- Salt and black pepper to taste
- Grated Parmesan cheese (for serving)

Instructions:

Cook the fettuccine according to the package instructions in a large pot of salted boiling water. Reserve about 1 cup of pasta cooking water before draining.
In a large skillet, heat olive oil over medium-high heat. Add finely chopped shallot and sauté until it becomes translucent.
Add minced garlic to the skillet and sauté for about 1-2 minutes until fragrant.
Pour in dry white wine, scraping up any browned bits from the bottom of the skillet. Allow the wine to simmer and reduce by half.
Add heavy cream to the skillet, stirring continuously. Bring the mixture to a simmer.
Toss the sliced smoked salmon into the skillet, allowing it to heat through in the creamy sauce.
Stir in the zest and juice of one lemon, along with chopped fresh dill. Season with salt and black pepper to taste.
Toss the cooked and drained fettuccine into the skillet, coating it evenly with the Smoked Salmon and Dill sauce. If needed, add a bit of the reserved pasta cooking water to achieve the desired consistency.
Serve the Smoked Salmon and Dill Pasta hot, optionally sprinkled with grated Parmesan cheese.

Enjoy your elegant and delicious Smoked Salmon and Dill Pasta!

Spaghetti with Clams

Ingredients:

- 8 oz (225g) spaghetti
- 2 pounds (900g) fresh clams, scrubbed and cleaned
- 3 tablespoons olive oil
- 4 cloves garlic, thinly sliced
- 1/2 teaspoon red pepper flakes (optional, for heat)
- 1 cup dry white wine
- 1/2 cup fresh parsley, chopped
- Salt and black pepper to taste
- Lemon wedges (for serving)

Instructions:

Cook the spaghetti according to the package instructions in a large pot of salted boiling water. Reserve about 1 cup of pasta cooking water before draining.
In a large skillet, heat olive oil over medium heat. Add thinly sliced garlic and red pepper flakes (if using). Sauté for about 1-2 minutes until the garlic is just golden, being careful not to burn it.
Add the cleaned clams to the skillet, stirring to coat them with the garlic and oil. Pour in the dry white wine, cover the skillet, and simmer for 5-7 minutes or until the clams have opened. Discard any clams that do not open.
Season the clam mixture with salt and black pepper to taste. Stir in the chopped fresh parsley.
Toss the cooked and drained spaghetti into the skillet, coating it evenly with the Clams, Garlic, and White Wine sauce. If needed, add a bit of the reserved pasta cooking water to achieve the desired consistency.
Serve the Spaghetti with Clams hot, garnished with additional fresh parsley and lemon wedges on the side.

Enjoy your delicious and authentic Spaghetti with Clams!

Sun-Dried Tomato and Basil Pesto Pasta

Ingredients:

- 8 oz (225g) penne or your favorite pasta
- 1 cup sun-dried tomatoes (packed in oil), drained
- 2 cups fresh basil leaves, packed
- 1/2 cup grated Parmesan cheese
- 1/4 cup pine nuts, toasted
- 2 cloves garlic, minced
- 1/2 cup extra-virgin olive oil
- Salt and black pepper to taste
- Grated Pecorino Romano cheese (for serving)
- Fresh basil leaves (for garnish)

Instructions:

Cook the penne according to the package instructions in a large pot of salted boiling water. Reserve about 1 cup of pasta cooking water before draining.

In a food processor, combine the drained sun-dried tomatoes, fresh basil, grated Parmesan cheese, toasted pine nuts, and minced garlic. Pulse until the ingredients are finely chopped.

With the food processor running, gradually pour in the extra-virgin olive oil until the mixture becomes a smooth pesto. If the pesto is too thick, you can add more olive oil or some reserved pasta cooking water.

Season the pesto with salt and black pepper to taste. Pulse a few more times to incorporate the seasoning.

Toss the cooked and drained penne into a bowl, coating it evenly with the Sun-Dried Tomato and Basil Pesto.

Serve the pasta hot, garnished with grated Pecorino Romano cheese and fresh basil leaves.

Enjoy your vibrant and delicious Sun-Dried Tomato and Basil Pesto Pasta!

Beef and Mushroom Stuffed Shells

Ingredients:

For the Stuffed Shells:

- 20 jumbo pasta shells
- 1 pound (450g) ground beef
- 8 oz (225g) mushrooms, finely chopped
- 1 small onion, finely chopped
- 2 cloves garlic, minced
- 1 cup ricotta cheese
- 1 cup shredded mozzarella cheese
- 1/2 cup grated Parmesan cheese
- 1 egg
- 2 tablespoons fresh parsley, chopped
- Salt and black pepper to taste

For Baking:

- 2 cups marinara sauce
- 1 cup shredded mozzarella cheese
- Chopped fresh parsley (for garnish)

Instructions:

Cook the jumbo pasta shells according to the package instructions in a large pot of salted boiling water. Drain and set aside.

In a skillet, cook the ground beef over medium-high heat until browned. Drain any excess fat.

Add chopped mushrooms, finely chopped onion, and minced garlic to the skillet. Sauté until the mushrooms release their moisture and the vegetables are softened. Allow the mixture to cool.

In a large bowl, combine the cooked beef and mushroom mixture with ricotta cheese, shredded mozzarella cheese, grated Parmesan cheese, egg, chopped fresh parsley, salt, and black pepper. Mix until well combined.

Preheat the oven to 375°F (190°C).

Stuff each cooked pasta shell with the beef and mushroom mixture.

Spread a thin layer of marinara sauce in the bottom of a baking dish.

Arrange the stuffed shells in the baking dish. Pour the remaining marinara sauce over the shells.
Sprinkle shredded mozzarella cheese over the top.
Cover the baking dish with foil and bake in the preheated oven for 25-30 minutes or until the cheese is melted and bubbly.
Remove the foil and bake for an additional 5-10 minutes, allowing the cheese to brown.
Garnish with chopped fresh parsley before serving.

Enjoy your delicious and hearty Beef and Mushroom Stuffed Shells!

Lemon Asparagus Orzo

Ingredients:

- 8 oz (225g) orzo pasta
- 1 bunch fresh asparagus, trimmed and cut into bite-sized pieces
- 2 tablespoons olive oil
- 3 cloves garlic, minced
- Zest and juice of 2 lemons
- 1/2 cup grated Parmesan cheese
- Salt and black pepper to taste
- Red pepper flakes (optional, for heat)
- Fresh parsley, chopped (for garnish)

Instructions:

Cook the orzo according to the package instructions in a large pot of salted boiling water. About 2 minutes before the orzo is done, add the bite-sized asparagus pieces to the boiling water. Cook until the orzo is al dente and the asparagus is tender-crisp. Drain and set aside.

In a large skillet, heat olive oil over medium heat. Add minced garlic and sauté for about 1 minute until fragrant.

Add the cooked orzo and asparagus to the skillet, tossing to coat in the garlic-infused oil.

Zest and juice the lemons directly into the skillet, stirring to combine.

Sprinkle grated Parmesan cheese over the orzo and asparagus, tossing until the cheese is melted and the ingredients are well combined.

Season with salt, black pepper, and red pepper flakes (if using), adjusting to taste.

Garnish with chopped fresh parsley before serving.

Enjoy your light and flavorful Lemon Asparagus Orzo! This dish is perfect for a quick and refreshing meal.

Pappardelle with Wild Mushroom Sauce

Ingredients:

- 12 oz (340g) pappardelle pasta
- 2 tablespoons olive oil
- 1/2 cup shallots, finely chopped
- 3 cloves garlic, minced
- 1 pound (450g) mixed wild mushrooms (such as cremini, shiitake, oyster), cleaned and sliced
- 1/2 cup dry white wine
- 1 cup chicken or vegetable broth
- 1 cup heavy cream
- Salt and black pepper to taste
- 1/4 cup fresh parsley, chopped
- Grated Parmesan cheese (for serving)

Instructions:

Cook the pappardelle pasta according to the package instructions in a large pot of salted boiling water. Reserve about 1 cup of pasta cooking water before draining.

In a large skillet, heat olive oil over medium-high heat. Add finely chopped shallots and sauté until they become translucent.

Add minced garlic to the skillet and sauté for about 1-2 minutes until fragrant.

Add the sliced wild mushrooms to the skillet, cooking until they release their moisture and become golden brown.

Pour in the dry white wine, scraping up any browned bits from the bottom of the skillet. Allow the wine to simmer and reduce by half.

Add chicken or vegetable broth to the skillet, stirring to combine. Allow it to simmer for a few minutes.

Stir in the heavy cream, bringing the mixture to a gentle simmer. Cook until the sauce thickens.

Season the sauce with salt and black pepper to taste.

Toss the cooked and drained pappardelle into the skillet, coating it evenly with the Wild Mushroom Sauce. If needed, add a bit of the reserved pasta cooking water to achieve the desired consistency.

Serve the Pappardelle with Wild Mushroom Sauce hot, garnished with chopped fresh parsley and grated Parmesan cheese.

Enjoy your luxurious and flavorful Pappardelle with Wild Mushroom Sauce!

Spaghetti Carbonara with Pancetta

Ingredients:

- 12 oz (340g) spaghetti
- 1 cup pancetta, diced
- 2 tablespoons olive oil
- 3 large eggs
- 1 cup grated Pecorino Romano cheese (or Parmesan), plus extra for serving
- Salt and black pepper to taste
- 2 cloves garlic, minced (optional)
- Fresh parsley, chopped (for garnish)

Instructions:

Cook the spaghetti according to the package instructions in a large pot of salted boiling water. Reserve about 1 cup of pasta cooking water before draining.
In a large skillet, heat olive oil over medium heat. Add diced pancetta and cook until it becomes crispy and golden brown.
If using minced garlic, add it to the skillet and sauté for about 1 minute until fragrant.
In a bowl, whisk together the eggs and grated Pecorino Romano cheese until well combined.
When the spaghetti is cooked, drain it and immediately toss it into the skillet with the crispy pancetta. Remove the skillet from heat.
Quickly pour the egg and cheese mixture over the hot pasta, tossing vigorously to coat the spaghetti and create a creamy sauce. If the sauce is too thick, add some of the reserved pasta cooking water gradually until you reach the desired consistency.
Season the Carbonara with salt and black pepper to taste.
Garnish with chopped fresh parsley and extra grated Pecorino Romano cheese.
Serve the Spaghetti Carbonara with Pancetta immediately while it's warm.

Enjoy your delicious and authentic Spaghetti Carbonara with Pancetta!

Creamy Tomato Basil Penne

Ingredients:

- 8 oz (225g) penne pasta
- 2 tablespoons olive oil
- 1 small onion, finely chopped
- 2 cloves garlic, minced
- 1 can (14 oz) crushed tomatoes
- 1/2 cup heavy cream
- 1 teaspoon dried oregano
- 1 teaspoon dried basil
- Salt and black pepper to taste
- 1/4 teaspoon red pepper flakes (optional, for heat)
- 1/4 cup fresh basil, chopped
- Grated Parmesan cheese (for serving)

Instructions:

Cook the penne pasta according to the package instructions in a large pot of salted boiling water. Reserve about 1 cup of pasta cooking water before draining.
In a large skillet, heat olive oil over medium heat. Add finely chopped onion and sauté until it becomes translucent.
Add minced garlic to the skillet and sauté for about 1-2 minutes until fragrant.
Pour in the crushed tomatoes, dried oregano, and dried basil. Simmer the sauce for about 10 minutes, allowing it to thicken.
Stir in the heavy cream, red pepper flakes (if using), salt, and black pepper. Simmer for an additional 5 minutes.
Toss the cooked and drained penne into the skillet, coating it evenly with the Creamy Tomato Basil sauce. If needed, add a bit of the reserved pasta cooking water to achieve the desired consistency.
Stir in the chopped fresh basil, reserving some for garnish.
Serve the Creamy Tomato Basil Penne hot, garnished with additional fresh basil and grated Parmesan cheese.

Enjoy your flavorful and creamy Tomato Basil Penne!

Chicken and Spinach Lasagna

Ingredients:

For the Filling:

- 9 lasagna noodles, cooked according to package instructions
- 2 cups cooked and shredded chicken breast
- 4 cups fresh spinach, chopped
- 1 cup ricotta cheese
- 1 cup shredded mozzarella cheese
- 1/2 cup grated Parmesan cheese
- 2 cloves garlic, minced
- 1 egg
- Salt and black pepper to taste

For the Béchamel Sauce:

- 4 tablespoons unsalted butter
- 1/4 cup all-purpose flour
- 4 cups milk
- Salt and nutmeg to taste

Instructions:

Preheat the oven to 375°F (190°C).

In a large mixing bowl, combine the shredded chicken, chopped spinach, ricotta cheese, shredded mozzarella, grated Parmesan, minced garlic, and egg. Mix well. Season with salt and black pepper to taste.

In a saucepan, melt the butter over medium heat for the béchamel sauce. Add the flour and whisk continuously until it forms a smooth paste.

Gradually pour in the milk while whisking to prevent lumps. Continue whisking until the sauce thickens.

Season the béchamel sauce with salt and a pinch of nutmeg to taste. Remove from heat.

In a baking dish, spread a thin layer of béchamel sauce.

Place a layer of cooked lasagna noodles over the béchamel sauce.

Spread a portion of the chicken and spinach mixture evenly over the noodles.

Pour a generous amount of béchamel sauce over the chicken and spinach layer.

Repeat the process, layering lasagna noodles, chicken and spinach mixture, and béchamel sauce until you finish with a layer of béchamel sauce on top.
Sprinkle extra shredded mozzarella and grated Parmesan cheese on the top layer.
Bake in the preheated oven for about 25-30 minutes or until the top is golden and bubbly.
Allow the Chicken and Spinach Lasagna to cool for a few minutes before slicing.
Garnish with fresh parsley or basil if desired.

Enjoy your delicious and creamy Chicken and Spinach Lasagna!

Broccoli and Cheddar Stuffed Shells

Ingredients:

- 20 jumbo pasta shells
- 2 cups broccoli florets, steamed and chopped
- 1 1/2 cups shredded cheddar cheese
- 1 cup ricotta cheese
- 1/2 cup grated Parmesan cheese
- 1 large egg
- 2 cloves garlic, minced
- 1/2 teaspoon dried oregano
- Salt and black pepper to taste

For the Sauce:

- 2 cups marinara sauce
- 1 cup shredded mozzarella cheese (for topping)
- Fresh parsley, chopped (for garnish)

Instructions:

Preheat the oven to 375°F (190°C).
Cook the jumbo pasta shells according to the package instructions in a large pot of salted boiling water. Drain and set aside.
In a large mixing bowl, combine chopped steamed broccoli, shredded cheddar cheese, ricotta cheese, grated Parmesan cheese, egg, minced garlic, dried oregano, salt, and black pepper. Mix until well combined.
In a baking dish, spread a thin layer of marinara sauce.
Stuff each cooked pasta shell with the broccoli and cheddar mixture, placing them in the baking dish.
Pour the remaining marinara sauce over the stuffed shells.
Sprinkle shredded mozzarella cheese over the top.
Cover the baking dish with foil and bake in the preheated oven for 20-25 minutes.
Remove the foil and bake for an additional 5-10 minutes or until the cheese is melted and bubbly.
Garnish with chopped fresh parsley before serving.

Enjoy your cheesy and flavorful Broccoli and Cheddar Stuffed Shells!

Caramelized Onion and Goat Cheese Linguine

Ingredients:

- 8 oz (225g) linguine or your favorite pasta
- 2 large onions, thinly sliced
- 2 tablespoons olive oil
- 2 tablespoons balsamic vinegar
- 4 oz (113g) goat cheese
- Salt and black pepper to taste
- Fresh thyme leaves (for garnish)
- Grated Parmesan cheese (optional, for serving)

Instructions:

Cook the linguine according to the package instructions in a large pot of salted boiling water. Reserve about 1 cup of pasta cooking water before draining.

While the pasta is cooking, heat olive oil in a large skillet over medium-low heat. Add the thinly sliced onions and cook, stirring occasionally, until the onions become soft and golden brown, about 20-25 minutes.

Add balsamic vinegar to the caramelized onions, stirring to coat them. Continue to cook for an additional 5 minutes until the vinegar is absorbed.

Crumble the goat cheese into the skillet with the caramelized onions, stirring until the cheese is melted and forms a creamy sauce.

Season the sauce with salt and black pepper to taste.

Toss the cooked and drained linguine into the skillet, coating it evenly with the Caramelized Onion and Goat Cheese sauce. If needed, add a bit of the reserved pasta cooking water to achieve the desired consistency.

Serve the Caramelized Onion and Goat Cheese Linguine hot, garnished with fresh thyme leaves and optionally sprinkled with grated Parmesan cheese.

Enjoy your flavorful and creamy Caramelized Onion and Goat Cheese Linguine!

Shrimp and Lobster Linguine

Ingredients:

- 8 oz (225g) linguine or your favorite pasta
- 1 lobster tail, cooked and meat removed, chopped
- 8 oz (225g) large shrimp, peeled and deveined
- 2 tablespoons olive oil
- 3 cloves garlic, minced
- 1/2 cup dry white wine
- 1 cup cherry tomatoes, halved
- 1/2 cup heavy cream
- 1/4 cup grated Parmesan cheese
- Salt and black pepper to taste
- Fresh parsley, chopped (for garnish)
- Lemon wedges (for serving)

Instructions:

Cook the linguine according to the package instructions in a large pot of salted boiling water. Reserve about 1 cup of pasta cooking water before draining.
In a large skillet, heat olive oil over medium-high heat. Add minced garlic and sauté for about 1 minute until fragrant.
Add the chopped lobster meat and peeled shrimp to the skillet. Cook until the shrimp turn pink and the lobster is heated through.
Pour in the dry white wine, stirring to deglaze the skillet. Allow the wine to simmer and reduce by half.
Add halved cherry tomatoes to the skillet, cooking until they soften.
Lower the heat and pour in the heavy cream, stirring to combine. Simmer for a few minutes until the sauce thickens.
Stir in grated Parmesan cheese, season with salt and black pepper to taste.
Toss the cooked and drained linguine into the skillet, coating it evenly with the Shrimp and Lobster sauce. If needed, add a bit of the reserved pasta cooking water to achieve the desired consistency.
Serve the Shrimp and Lobster Linguine hot, garnished with chopped fresh parsley and lemon wedges on the side.

Enjoy your decadent and delicious Shrimp and Lobster Linguine!

Spicy Arrabbiata Pasta

Ingredients:

- 8 oz (225g) penne or your favorite pasta
- 2 tablespoons olive oil
- 4 cloves garlic, minced
- 1/2 teaspoon red pepper flakes (adjust to taste)
- 1 can (28 oz) crushed tomatoes
- 1 teaspoon dried oregano
- 1 teaspoon dried basil
- Salt to taste
- Black pepper to taste
- Fresh basil, chopped (for garnish)
- Grated Parmesan cheese (optional, for serving)

Instructions:

Cook the penne according to the package instructions in a large pot of salted boiling water. Reserve about 1 cup of pasta cooking water before draining.

In a large skillet, heat olive oil over medium heat. Add minced garlic and red pepper flakes. Sauté for about 1 minute until the garlic is fragrant.

Pour in the crushed tomatoes, dried oregano, and dried basil. Simmer the sauce for about 15-20 minutes, allowing it to thicken.

Season the Arrabbiata sauce with salt and black pepper to taste. Adjust the level of red pepper flakes according to your desired spiciness.

Toss the cooked and drained penne into the skillet, coating it evenly with the Spicy Arrabbiata sauce. If needed, add a bit of the reserved pasta cooking water to achieve the desired consistency.

Serve the Spicy Arrabbiata Pasta hot, garnished with chopped fresh basil. Optionally, sprinkle with grated Parmesan cheese.

Enjoy your bold and spicy Arrabbiata Pasta!

Creamy Pumpkin Alfredo

Ingredients:

- 8 oz (225g) fettuccine or your favorite pasta
- 2 tablespoons unsalted butter
- 2 cloves garlic, minced
- 1 cup canned pumpkin puree
- 1 cup heavy cream
- 1/2 cup grated Parmesan cheese
- 1/4 teaspoon ground nutmeg
- Salt and black pepper to taste
- Chopped fresh sage (for garnish)
- Grated Pecorino Romano cheese (optional, for serving)

Instructions:

Cook the fettuccine according to the package instructions in a large pot of salted boiling water. Reserve about 1 cup of pasta cooking water before draining.

In a large skillet, melt unsalted butter over medium heat. Add minced garlic and sauté for about 1-2 minutes until fragrant.

Stir in the canned pumpkin puree, heavy cream, grated Parmesan cheese, ground nutmeg, salt, and black pepper. Continue to cook, stirring frequently, until the sauce is heated through and well combined.

Toss the cooked and drained fettuccine into the skillet, coating it evenly with the Creamy Pumpkin Alfredo sauce. If needed, add a bit of the reserved pasta cooking water to achieve the desired consistency.

Serve the Creamy Pumpkin Alfredo hot, garnished with chopped fresh sage. Optionally, sprinkle with grated Pecorino Romano cheese.

Enjoy your cozy and flavorful Creamy Pumpkin Alfredo!